O Rare Ralph McInerny

Other titles from St. Augustine's Press & Dumb Ox Books

Written by Ralph McInerny

Some Catholic Writers
The Defamation of Pius XII
Good Knights: Eight Stories
Shakespearean Variations
The Soul of Wit
Let's Read Latin

Translation by Ralph McInerny

John of St. Thomas, *Introduction to the Summa Theologiae of Thomas Aquinas*
Thomas Aquinas, *Disputed Questions on Virtue*
Florent Gaboriau, *The Conversion of Edith Stein*

Introduction or Preface by Ralph McInerny

Thomas Aquinas, *Commentary on Aristotle's De Anima*
Thomas Aquinas, *Commentary on Aristotle's Metaphysics*
Thomas Aquinas, *Commentary on Aristotle's Nicomachean Ethics*
Thomas Aquinas, *Commentary on Aristotle's Physics*
Thomas Aquinas, *Commentary on Aristotle's Posterior Analytics*
Charles E. Rice, *What Happened to Notre Dame?*
Fulvio di Blasi, *God and the Natural Law*

Other Titles of Interest

James V. Schall, *The Regensburg Lecture*
Josef Pieper, *Happiness and Contemplation*
Josef Pieper, *The Silence of St. Thomas*
Josef Pieper, *What Catholics Believe*
C.S. Lewis, *The Latin Letters of C.S. Lewis*
Rémi Brague, *Eccentric Culture: A Theory of Western Civilization*
Peter Kreeft, *The Philosophy of Jesus*
Jacques Maritain, *Natural Law: Reflections on Theory and Practice*
Gabriel Marcel, *The Mystery of Being* (in two volumes)
Gabriel Marcel, *Thou Shall Not Die*

O Rare Ralph McInerny

Stories and Reflections about a Legendary Notre Dame Professor

With Parting Words from the Honoree

Edited and Introduced by Christopher Kaczor

ST. AUGUSTINE'S PRESS
South Bend, Indiana

Manufactured in the United States of America

1 2 3 4 5 6   16 15 14 13 12 11

Library of Congress Cataloging in Publication Data
O Rare Ralph McInerny : stories and reflections about a legendary Notre Dame professor, with parting words from the honoree / edited and introduced by Christopher Kaczor.
p. cm.
Includes bibliographical references and index.
ISBN 978-1-58731-585-5 (pbk.: alk. paper) 1. McInerny, Ralph, 1929–2010. 2. Authors, American – 20th century – Biography. 3. Catholic authors – United States – Biography. 4. College teachers – United States – Biography. 5. McInerny, Ralph, 1929–2010 – Bibliography. I. Kaczor, Christopher Robert, 1969–
PS3563.A31166Z8 2010
813'.54 – dc22   [B]   2010027390

∞ The paper used in this publication meets the minimum requirements of the American National Standard for Information Sciences – Permanence of Paper for Printed Materials, ANSI Z39.48-1984.

ST. AUGUSTINE'S PRESS
www.staugustine.net

Dedicated to
Alice Osberger.

Thank You
From All of Us

Contents

Introduction

Ralph Magis McInerny

I realize his middle name was Matthew, but it might as well have been *Magis*, Latin for "more." He taught for more than 50 years, wrote more than 50 books in philosophy and other disciplines, penned more than a thousand essays, short stories, columns, and poems, authored more than 90 fiction books, and directed more dissertations than anyone in the history of Notre Dame. When I mentioned to my mother that his funeral included 28 priests and a military color guard playing taps because he was also a Marine, she responded, "Is there anything that man didn't do?"

His academic achievements are well known—eight honorary doctorates, presidential and pontifical appointments, Gifford Lectures, and teaching stints from Argentina to Oxford. His man was, of course, St. Thomas Aquinas, but not only Thomas. The *New York Times* obituary noted that Ralph "wrote on the sixth-century philosopher Boethius, the 12th-century Spanish Arabic scholar Averroes and later thinkers and theologians, including Cardinal Newman, Kierkegaard, Pascal and Descartes." The *Los Angeles Times* obituary focused on him as "the prolific author of approximately 100 novels. Beginning with 'Her Death of Cold' in 1977, he wrote more than two dozen mysteries featuring Father Dowling, which led to the 1989–91 'Father Dowling Mysteries' TV series starring Tom Bosley." Indeed, *The Times* of London was not the first place to note Ralph's extraordinary productivity. "George Orwell, who famously, and wrongly, concluded that the Billy Bunter oeuvre was too vast to have been written by one man (Frank Richards), would have had a similar problem with the output of Ralph McInerny, the American Catholic scholar and writer of detective fiction." But Ralph was much more than a prolific author.

This book aims to capture some of the "more" that was McInerny, a more that cannot be captured by any *curriculum vitae*, even one as impressive as Ralph's. The stories and anecdotes in this volume give us various snapshots of the man that cannot be found in obituaries or press releases. A man as great as Ralph should not live merely in memory, so some record such as this volume becomes appropriate. His brother, life-long friends, colleagues, and a small selection of his doctoral students have come together to gather their thoughts and their thanksgiving to Ralph in this book.

Part of the more—unquantifiable but no less real—was how Ralph treated people and how they responded to him. Among his students, he commanded universal respect. In this absence, other professors were called by their last name, Jordan, Gersh, Van Engen, but Ralph was always spoken of as 'Dr. McInerny.' One might think such a prolific author would neglect his students; *au contraire* (a McInerny habit was to end sentences in academic lectures in Latin or French). He was my dissertation advisor and at the time he had around eight other students, as well. He was available for us virtually every afternoon in his seventh floor office in the Jacque Maritain Center, located in Hesburgh Library. If we gave him a dissertation chapter, he'd have it back to us like a serve in tennis (a line from Thurber that Ralph liked to quote). He gave us laptops. He arranged for extra funding (many of us had two or three kids, and none of us made more than $10,000 a year). He took us out to lunch (The Great Wall of China and the University Club were favorites). He'd give us copies of his scholarly books and his mystery novels. He helped get us jobs. Most of all perhaps, he provided a living model of a philosopher, a mentor, and a man who embodied virtues and commitments that inspired us all.

Ralph's was teaching assistant for his undergraduate course "The Thought of Aquinas," which was my first class in Thomistic thought. During my undergraduate days at Boston College, I had been assigned to read Karl Marx in three different courses, but was never once given a page of St. Thomas. Ralph taught me—in that class and also in his many books—a great deal about the relationship of faith and reason, about ethics, and about God. More importantly, he prompted me to fall in love with Aquinas. It was also there I first heard the words, words he loved to repeat, from the French writer Leon Bloy, "There is only one tragedy in life: not being a saint." Though not without moments of deep sadness, Ralph's life was no tragedy. Indeed his work, his friends, and his faith gave him a joy that radiated to others.

Ralph's *joie de vivre* manifested itself in a ready smile and a quick wit. Even from his youth, he delighted those around him. In his autobiography, *I Alone Have Escaped to Tell You*, he writes about being in first grade and not yet having mastered the mystery of R. "My teacher, Sister Mary Electa, would take me up the hall to the other nuns, and I would be put through a little ritual. What is your name? Walph. What are your brothers' names? Woger and Waymond. There was nothing cruel in this; they obviously found my lisping cute, and I would be hugged and taken back to my desk." The *UK Telegraph* noted, "An inveterate punster, he liked to give his mystery novels titles like *Body and Soil, Frigor Mortis* and *Law and Ardour*. One of his books on St Thomas Aquinas was subtitled *A Handbook for Peeping Thomists*." To those titles, we could add many others, such as *Mom and Dead, Celt and Pepper, Good Knights,* and *Lack of the Irish* (a book he kindly dedicated to my wife Jennifer and me). When he was still in his 60s, Ralph joked to me about his mortality, "I no longer buy green bananas." About a host who did not leave him any time for himself, "He's rather adhesive." About what he would like to say to a scholar with prolific but narrowly focused writing, "I see you have another book out. What are you calling it this time?"

He called forth the best from us by seeing it in us before we did. After a lunch at Antoine's in New Orleans with Mortimer Adler, Ralph wrote, "I felt like a rustic nephew being treated by a rich and cosmopolitan uncle." Around Ralph, I always felt like that rustic nephew, with the addition of a speech impediment. Whether it was in my doctoral comprehensive exams, a public lecture (at his invitation) at Notre Dame, or at a talk at the

Gregorian in Rome, he had the habit of sitting in the front row and asking the first question of me, which I never failed to fumble. Nevertheless, he seemed to abound in invitations. Once when he was going to be absent, he asked me to guest teach the Ph.D. graduate seminar I was taking from him. He invited me to work with him on various projects including as an assistant editor of *Catholic Dossier*, a copy editor of Maritain's *Degrees of Knowledge*, a board member of the International Catholic University, and a co-author with him of *An Illustrated Life of Aquinas* (a rare uncompleted project). He was the first scholar to cite me in print, and for some time I thought he'd also be the last. He was so extraordinarily kind that I told my wife he must be the uncle of my Minneapolis-born birth mother whom I had not yet met.

Days before my dissertation defense in 1996, Ralph had to undergo emergency triple bypass surgery (I claim there was no causal connection). I thought he would miss the graduation ceremony. But there he was, a few weeks later, ashen and weak, but ready to put the doctoral hood over me as well as John O'Callaghan who would later succeed him as Director of the Jacque Maritain Center.

After graduation, he'd gather his former doctoral students, a sizable *Schulerkreis*, back together for Summer Thomistic Institutes at Notre Dame along with an international cast of young, mid-level and senior scholars. Inspired by Jacques Maritain's *Cercle d'Études*, Ralph gave us a forum in which spiritual growth and intellectual pursuits fed each other in a context of camaraderie. It was there that we presented our research, made important professional contacts, and deepened our friendship with him and each other. We prayed together, sang together, ate together, and talked late into the night. He, and Alice Osberger his longtime administrative assistant, made it all happen—all at no cost to us.

No doubt Ralph is enjoying his reward, meeting his Maker and, as an incidental benefit, his own model of the intellectual life, Thomas Aquinas. When I think about how I hope to live the rest of my life, he is the model: scholar, teacher, writer, family man, person of faith. This book is a small snapshot of the more that was McInerny.

Christopher Kaczor is Professor of Philosophy at Loyola Marymount University in Los Angeles. He is also the author of *Thomas Aquinas on Faith, Hope, and Love*, *The Ethics of Abortion: Women's Rights, Human Life, and the Question of Justice*, *How to Stay Catholic in College*, *Life Issues, Medical Choices* (with Janet Smith), and *Thomas Aquinas on the Cardinal Virtues* (with Thomas Sherman, S.J.).

Memories of Lake Johanna

Nineteen-forty-eight was a year full of interest. Harry Truman surprised all the political pundits and was elected President in his own right. Congress enacted the Marshall Plan, just as the Communists seized control of Czechoslovakia. Israel, after a fierce struggle, attained its statehood, which has endured, and Chiang-Kai-shek attained the presidency of China, which has not. Among the famous people who died in 1948, two were of legendary caliber, though for very different reasons: Mohandas Gandhi, who fasted his nation into independence, was assassinated, and Babe Ruth, for whom the word "fast" had meaning only in distinction to the word "curve," was consumed by his own exuberant appetites. Olivier's *Hamlet* won the Academy Award that year, and Cole Porter's *Kiss Me, Kate*, a rather more rollicking exposure to Shakespeare, was the smash hit on Broadway. Martin Buber's *Moses* was published, and so was Alfred Kinsey's *Sexual Behavior in the Human Male*—one of them was a best-seller. Eddie Arcaro, on "Citation," won the triple crown of racing, and the Nobel Prize for Literature went to T. S. Eliot.

For those of us who lived in Minnesota, 1948 had some special moments. During the summer Hubert Humphrey, mayor of Minneapolis, a delegate to the Democratic National Convention, sponsored a strong civil rights plank for the party's platform, the adoption of which led to the secession of the so-called Dixiecrats under the leadership of Strom Thurmond of South Carolina; in November Mayor Humphrey became Senator Humphrey. In that same general election Eugene McCarthy, a sociology instructor at the College of St. Thomas in St. Paul, won the local seat in the House of Representatives. All three men ran for the presidency at one time or another, and all three fell short. Now, fifty-one years later, Mr. Humphrey has long since been honorably gathered to his fathers; Mr. Thurmond, having exchanged his white sheet for a ginger-colored hair-piece, dozes through his days as president pro tem of the United States Senate; and Mr. McCarthy, having relinquished his status as eccentric activist politician, writes poetry of unremarkable quality from his retreat in northern Virginia. Such are the vagaries of time.

By 1948 Ralph McInerny had returned to Arden Hills. Actually, he had returned the previous autumn, but I choose to focus on 1948, because that was the year our friendship began and ripened. And anyway he keeps returning to that treasured place in his mind and heart and imagination. Listen to this description of a pilgrimage made by a fictional character who, like Ralph himself, had long since departed and yet could not stay away. "He drove out Snelling Avenue, and then he saw the great square tower lift above the trees. He did not try to stop the pang of painful pleasure the sight of it gave him. He took the next exit and turned onto Juniper, following it beneath the freeway he had been on, a shaded tunnel on the other side of which, almost immediately, was the entrance gate. What had once been a dirt road through the woods was blacktopped now and lined with new buildings, alien structures that distorted his memories. Even when he came in sight of the original building, it was difficult to regain the stab of nostalgia he had felt at the sight of the tower. But once he had parked and got out of the car, with Nazareth Hall on his left and the lake on his right, he felt that he had been transported back into the land of his youth. *Introibo ad altare Dei; ad Deum qui laetificat iuventutem meam.* I shall go in unto the altar of God, the God who gives joy to my youth." This passage is taken from Ralph's novel, *The Red Hat*, which he completed only two years ago.

Arden Hills today is a rather posh suburb at the northern edge of St. Paul. In 1948, however, it was still a rural area of farms and woodland, dotted here and there by small and charming lakes. On a peninsula thrusting into three shores of one of these lakes, Johanna by name, the archdiocese of St. Paul, since 1923, had maintained its minor seminary. It was housed in an imposingly large and exquisite building, brooded over by a great Norman tower, constructed L-shaped in the Italian style, with a vast red-tiled roof and a pillared loggia running across the front. Upon a tiny island to the east, linked to the mainland by a wooden walking-bridge, stood a pretty little structure which, the local lore had it, was the mausoleum of a benefactress of the institution, a *femme fatale* of some sort, who had been denied an ordinary Christian burial because she had drowned herself in Lake Michigan. Whatever the truth of this tale, the fact that the memorial always remained locked up tight added a certain piquancy to the lives of boys and young men ever ready to indulge in conspiracy theories.

On the main floor of the school-building were the conventional offices and classrooms, a modest auditorium, a science laboratory, a large and sunny refectory, and a chapel of quite breath-taking beauty, all multi-colored marble and dark wood, and with the façade of the tabernacle on the altar cunningly crafted so that its gold leaf would brighten when the rear doors opened and let in the light. Whenever I remember it, I catch a faint fragrance of incense. In a niche in the wall along the main corridor outside, was a tall granite statue of Jesus, the Boy of Nazareth, the *Puer Nazarenus*, his features carved in terms of dignity and compassion. Here most of us manifested a certain, I hope inculpable, superstition, as, when we passed by, we brushed a hand across the stone feet of the statue, hoping that our aspirations might be realized. We understood in any case the significance of the name of the school to which we had come: Nazareth Hall.

Below the chapel was a crypt, where individual altars were provided upon which the priest-professors celebrated daily Mass. At the other extremity of this basement floor was the cramped basketball court, cramped indeed, since at one end the out-of-bounds was indicated not by a line upon the floor but by the wall itself —I have the scars to prove it. The reason for this anomaly was that the original plan had called for this space to be a swimming pool when, predictably in projects undertaken by Catholics in those days, the money ran out. Contiguous to this unlikely gymnasium was a little store—we called it the "pie plant"—where, on Wednesday and Saturday afternoons, the only extended free periods we had, sweets and, most importantly, a half-pint of ice cream could be purchased.

At the far end of the L, prudently—indeed, as it seems now prudishly—quarantined from all the male precincts of the institution, stood the convent, with its own courtyard and chapel. The sisters who lived and worshipped there, all Germans and refugees from Nazi persecution, oversaw the kitchen and the infirmary. I'm confident that Ralph remembers them as I do—Mother Laura and Sisters Teatima and Turibia and the others—as sweet and good and consoling—and as lousy cooks. Grease seemed to be the essential ingredient of everything they prepared, from blueberry muffins in the morning to mystery loaf—as we came to dub the greyish lump composed of a weird combination of war-time rationed meat and wilted vegetables—they offered in the evening. At one point the rector, in hopes of ameliorating this situation, sent the nuns off to St. Louis to a conference devoted to institutional food preparation. Upon their return, Mother Laura responded to the rector's anxious inquiry with a brusque shake of her coifed head. "Ach, Monsignor," she said, "it was a waste of time. They don't do nothing the way we do."

Just to the west of the sisters' compound lay the football and softball fields—the latter converted by student muscle and endeavor into a hockey rink during the long Minnesota winters—as well as the volley ball and outside basketball courts and the horse-shoe pitches. And beyond these somewhat primitive facilities stretched the woods, almost the forest primeval, as it seemed to us. Hiking and games of capture the flag were marvelous diversions, and on one hilly clearing a toboggan slide had been built. The woods were alive too with small animals, which aroused little interest, and with a seemingly numberless variety of birds, which did. One of our priest-professors was a bird-watching enthusiast, and he was eager to share his hobby and his expertise with interested students. In fact, my oldest memory of Ralph goes back to a spring day in 1945 when this priest was pointing out to several of us freshmen a palliated sapsucker or some other exotic species, when a group of juniors ambled by. Once they had passed us I turned away from the less than fascinating disquisition in time to see Ralph grinning madly, rolling his eyes, and flapping his arms as though *he* were a palliated sapsucker.

Shortly after that Ralph departed Arden Hills. There was nothing unusual or unseemly about this. The minor seminary culture of those days, with its clientele composed of boys as young as fourteen, was designed to "test" a youngster's vocation to the priesthood, as the saying went, to provide him with an experience in which he could examine himself and his goals and talents, could ponder whether the work and life-style of a priest was in reality consonant with his adolescent perception of a calling from God. Ralph, having come to a decision in this regard, completed his secondary education at Cretin high school in St. Paul. (I must observe in passing that this institution received its unfortunate name because it was founded in memory of the first bishop of St. Paul, the Frenchman, Joseph Cretin, the pronunciation of whose surname was routinely anglicized; there was nothing cretinous about Cretin; indeed, it was, and is, a very good school.) After graduation Ralph joined the Marine Corps. I'm sure he did not during his brief tour of duty fire a weapon in anger, but surely it was not his fault that the enemies of democracy had already been vanquished. Within the salubrious confines of the base at San Diego at any rate, along with enduring the trials all servicemen are prey to, even in peacetime, he read a lot and thought a lot and, no doubt, prayed a lot. Once mustered out, he re-enrolled at Nazareth Hall.

Of course from his previous encounter he knew the drill. Nazareth Hall unabashedly purported to combine the ideals of the English public school and the French *petit séminaire*. The full course lasted six years, and Ralph now was registered as a college freshman—what we called a "fifth year man." There were about 250 students all told, who were in residence from early September till late May, with a lengthy holiday at Christmas time. High school students slept in dormitories, while college men shared small rooms in twos. Discipline was firm but fair; most infractions resulted in being "jugged," that is, assigned to do odd jobs during recreation periods. (I cannot tell you the origin of that peculiar term.) The rising bell rang at 6:00 a. m., 6:30 on Sundays. Traditional piety required that

that screeching noise be accompanied by a prefect shouting *Benedicamus Domino!*, to which the proper response was a thankful *Deo Gratias*; I'm proud to say that never in all my years did I give the proper response. Lights were to be turned off in the dormitories at 9:00 p.m. or 9:30, and in the college rooms a half-hour later.

Needless to say, religious and liturgical formalities occupied a good part of every day: meditation and low Mass each morning and a sumptuous sung Mass in addition on Sunday; recitation of the rosary or a lecture on asceticism delivered by the spiritual director in the late afternoon; and night prayers before retiring. Four confessors came from the outside each week, and there was a retreat, complete silence sternly enforced, once a year. The most difficult spiritual exercise imposed upon a fidgety youth was doubtless the so-called particular examen, held daily in chapel just before the noon meal; for an interminable five minutes he was expected to plumb his conscience in order to acknowledge failings committed since the day before due to his predominant fault, anger or envy or, perhaps with the hormones racing, lust. None of this, except for the examen, did we find onerous; after all what else should one have expected in a place like this? Of course every student responded inwardly in his own way, whatever outward manifestations he may have displayed.

Curiously, given the nature of the institution and its intense religiosity, the formal courses in religion were for the most part trivial and badly taught, almost, it seemed, a scholastic afterthought. Not so the rest of the curriculum. Classes met six mornings and four early afternoons each week. A student who passed through the entire gamut took six years of Latin, four of Greek, six of American and British literature, four of history, three of French or German, along with a solid introduction to the higher mathematics, theoretical physics, and laboratory chemistry. There were study periods every afternoon and evening. This regimen in the telling sounds excessively harsh, but in fact it was exhilarating. Maybe what made it attractive was the order and predictability of our lives, religious and scholastic. Maybe it was a special illumination that came to us during the annual retreat or during the stark performance of the Tenebrae on Holy Thursday night. Maybe it was the thrill of unraveling a difficult passage in Tacitus or Cicero, or the solemn moment when we read for ourselves, in Homer's own language, the description of the funeral rites for Hector, tamer of horses. And many of us still remember, over more than half a century, the resonant voice of our particularly gifted teacher of English literature reading Browning's *Andrea del Sarto* to us: "But do not let us quarrel any more,/ No, my Lucrezia; bear with me for once." In our physically confined little world, books became a focal point, and not only those examined in the classroom. On the second floor was the library, a small, wood-paneled room housing a collection modest by any reckoning, but embodying for us a mother lode of magic lore.

Maybe it was a combination of all these and many other related things that helped open the doors of mind and spirit. But basic to all else was a profound sense of comradeship. We were gathered together from a variety of backgrounds because we aspired to the same goal. Not only did we pray in company and struggle fruitlessly side by side to seek out our predominant fault. We all attended the same classes—the only elective was the choice between French and German—we all complained about the same greasy food, we all good naturedly mimicked the same professors, we all played the same games, some skillfully and some awkwardly, but, whatever the level of individual achievement and the score at the end, we recognized the competition as just one more binding tie. Smoking was allowed to fourth year men, high school seniors, and the collegians, but it was strictly forbidden inside the building—political correctness before its time. Behind the building, and attached to it, was a rickety wooden shed where tools were stored. This was our smoke shack, and every evening after supper we assembled there, puffed away, and sang together chorus after chorus, the harmonies of "Green Grow the Rushes Ho" and "My Darling Clementine" echoing across the fields and woods. Now lest you think these ruminations are merely the nostalgic meanderings of an old man looking back on the good old days—well, so they are. Of course Nazareth Hall in 1948 exhibited pettinesses and jealousies and bad humor and, sometimes, conflict and failure, as any institution or group of frail human beings is wont to do. It was, even so, a golden time.

And Ralph McInerny, on his second incarnation, became the center of our little community. Not only were we awe-struck at having an ex-Marine in our midst. He was bright and funny and accommodating in every way. He was interested in everything from politics to baseball to the structure of James Joyce's *Ulysses*, and he was willing to converse and even debate, without a trace of hubris, about anything. Even then he displayed that rare gift, so often exploited over the half century since, of holding firm views without being discourteous or disagreeable. He was always full of fun and that verbal facility—dreadful puns and all—for which he has become justly famous was already on display. When one of his classmates, Robert Senta by name, misbehaved in a French class, the instructor, an amiable but ineffectual fellow, made him take a seat in the front row. Ralph in the next half-hour whipped out a sonnet of several stanzas, each of which concluded with the line, "And Senta sits in front." In the satirical *Quid nunc* column that Ralph wrote for our internal mimeographed weekly, the *Puer Nazarenus*, he once referred this way to my ample derriere and the diminutive stature of a mutual friend: "*Quid* this week heard the rumor that a play is being composed by O'Connell and Klein, our very own Butt and Jeff."

Yes, Bob Klein and I were writing a play and lots of other quite forgettable pieces, not least because we wanted to follow Ralph's lead. But he was our mentor in a much more important sense. Consider first the time. The thirties, W. H. Auden's "low dishonest decade," were over. The war had been won, and, in its wake, the depression had passed away. It seemed a moment of rebirth had come, political and economic rebirth, to be sure, but an intellectual one as well. And consider next the place. An aging Sinclair Lewis may have seen his best days, but Minnesota meanwhile had given birth to Max Shulman, Thomas Heggen, and Sylvia Fine, and was bursting with literary vitality. We students cabined up at Nazareth Hall could not attend John Berryman's or Robert Penn Warren's lectures at the University of Minnesota, but we could read *The Dispossessed* and *All the King's Men*, and we did. And when Warren gave up his chair, he was succeeded by Allen Tate, author of the romantic "Ode to the Confederate Dead." We read the middle lines with awe: "Autumn is desolation in the plot/ Of a thousand acres where these memories grow/ From the inexhaustible bodies that are not/ Dead, but feed the grass row after rich row."

But Ralph grasped something more than the sheer beauty of this evocation of the Lost Cause. Allen Tate had joined the Catholic Church, as had his wife, the novelist Caroline Gordon. And so had their unruly friend, Robert Lowell, whose *Lord Weary's Castle* we read perhaps with more enthusiasm than comprehension. That mystical year 1948 presented to us Thomas Merton's *The Seven Storey Mountain*, the account of a wild and unpredictable conversion to Catholicism. We could not have known then of the succeeding years of love/hate Merton would experience with his Trappist vocation, or of his bizarre end in a bathtub in Thailand; we did know that here was another sign of a grand Catholic renaissance. Further evidence came simultaneously with the publication of the latest novel of another convert, Graham Greene's *The Heart of the Matter*, troubling perhaps in its theological implications, but nevertheless a testimony to the seriousness with which our religion was taken in the highest intellectual circles of the English-speaking world. Evelyn Waugh's spoof on the American way of death, *The Loved One*, contributed nothing to this conviction, but then *Brideshead Revisited* was only three years old in 1948, and what literary paean could have better revealed the sturdy endurance of our faith than this? The two poets we favored most, Eliot and Auden, were heretics, to be sure, but nice heretics, high Anglicans who professed belief in the Real Presence. And we greeted Eliot's elegant prose, in his *Notes Toward the Definition of Culture*, which also appeared in 1948, as though it had issued from Mount Olympus.

J. F. Powers, meanwhile, no convert he and now a Minnesotan, had begun to publish his incomparable clerical short stories, in which the "presence of grace"—his own term—battled with the all too human weaknesses of those priests who, we students at Nazareth Hall realized, might have been models of our future selves. And we had to wait for a little while until another born-Catholic, Flannery O'Connor of Milledgeville, Georgia, emerged.

In 1948, having passed through the prestigious writing programs at the University of Iowa and at Saratoga Springs, she was poised to bring her own gothic view of contemporary society, especially that of the southern United States, into the fullness of Catholic orthodoxy. The themes of her fiction were anything but explicit in this regard, but in her correspondence she made clear exactly where she stood. "I feel I can personally guarantee that St. Thomas loved God, because for the life of me I cannot help loving St. Thomas." The feeling here was more rigorous perhaps than the logic. But she went on: "His brothers didn't want him to waste himself being a Dominican and so locked him up in a tower and introduced a prostitute into his apartment. Her he ran out with a red-hot poker. It would be fashionable today to be in sympathy with the woman, but I am in sympathy with St. Thomas." More prosaic and direct was O'Connor's judgment about sophisticated analysis of the doctrine of the Eucharist: "If the consecrated Host is no more than a symbol, then I say to hell with it."

For Ralph McInerny, therefore, and for those of us at Nazareth Hall in 1948 who took our inspiration from him, this was an exalted moment. I don't believe that either he or we realized how profoundly significant the coupling of intellectual renewal and Catholic orthodoxy might prove to be in the long run. Ralph at any rate graduated from the Hall in the spring of 1949 and reported the following September to the major seminary, located in the heart of the city of St. Paul. To this venerable institution, founded in 1894, I followed him in the autumn of 1950. I discerned from the start of my renewed association that Ralph had undergone a conversion of his own, which, like the analogous religious experience, did not involve repudiating the good he already possessed, but rather adding another good to it. He did not lose his passion for literature, nor did he discard his intention to be a literary man himself. He did, however, like Flannery O'Connor, fall in love with St. Thomas Aquinas. I think the occasion for this new and rapturous preoccupation was the series of philosophy courses taught at the seminary by an extraordinarily able professor. This man, who also taught me to much less effect, had himself been a student of Charles de

Koninck, and so it was that Ralph was drawn into that vibrant Thomistic revival which centered at Laval University in Quebec. The results of that conversion are now part of a distinguished forty years of work, testified to by the books and articles, by the students taught and the dissertations directed and the offices splendidly administered, all of it brilliantly crowned so recently in Glasgow and again here, today, in his own university.

Ralph McInerny has long aroused wonder and envy at his demonstrated capacity to pursue with great success a literary as well as a philosophical career. I think I can shed some light on this puzzle. I think the roots of his accomplishment go back to 1948 and to Nazareth Hall. In that time and place, in the company, if I may say so without undue immodesty, of like-minded friends, he implicitly dedicated himself to the Catholic intellectual renaissance, the first evidences of which he found in the poems of Lowell and Tate, in the novels of Greene and Waugh, in the tortured odyssey of Thomas Merton. But the Laval circle too, by breathing new vigor into Thomism, formed an integral part of that renaissance. To embrace its values—to turn the mind's eye to the very texts of Aquinas rather than to manuals or commentators—did not mean deserting the earlier love. Quite to the contrary, it meant a fulfillment, a completion of a calling to the highest kind of service to God and his people. So flowing from his pen have been novels and stories and literary criticism of lofty quality, as well as learned treatises on analogy, being and predication, ethics, and a host of other philosophical subjects. Ralph McInerny proved it could be done, if one had the talent and the commitment to a great cause. And what strikes me as most remarkable, he has proceeded all these years less like an engineer along a double track than like a weaver spinning a seamless garment. I'm confident, however, that out of our old friendship Ralph will pardon me if I admit that I find a Father Dowling mystery more gripping than, say, *Aquinas Against the Averrroists*. Nor is it, incidentally, irrelevant to recall that Nazareth Hall was founded by a man named Dowling.

I trust that an exercise in nostalgia has not been out of place on such an occasion as this. Time, they say, heals all wounds, the stuff of forgetfulness, but it does not necessarily invalidate the aspirations of the past. "Your young men shall see visions," the prophet assures us, but "your old men shall dream dreams." The visions of 1948 have inevitably "gone whistling down the wind," to employ T. S. Eliot's melancholy phrase. Nazareth Hall is no more, or rather it has passed into alien hands which, out of ignorance rather than malice, have disfigured its former beauty and cluttered it round about with gimcrack construction. The *Puer Nazarenus* has disappeared from its niche, and the pews in the chapel have been painted a hideous white. Yet the dreams of today, rooted in those visions of a half century ago, live on, not least in the remarkable achievements of Ralph McInerny. Forgive me if, on this day when you have gathered to honor him as a philosopher, I prefer to remember those heady visions we shared along the shores of Lake Johanna so long ago. His dreams, to be sure, and ours, remain unfulfilled, and so they will continue to be until the last trumpet sounds. This should not surprise or disturb us. After all, "We are such stuff as dreams are made on, and our little life is rounded with a sleep."

Fr. Marvin R. O'Connell is Professor Emeritus of History at University of Notre Dame and the author of numerous books including Pilgrims to the Northland: The Archdiocese of St. Paul, 1840–1962, Edward Sorin, Blaise Pascal, *and* Critics on Trial: An Introduction to the Catholic Modernist Crisis. *These remarks were originally given on 4 December 1999 at the University of Notre Dame at the Banquet concluding "Recovering Nature," a conference to celebrate the life and career of Ralph McInerny.*

Fortiter in re, Suaviter in modo

Ralph McInerny was a friend and colleague throughout my four decades at Notre Dame. I was in the Law School, which was regarded by some as a trade school (personally, I take pride in that), and Ralph was "doing philosophy" in the upper regions of academia. Regrettably, lawyers and philosophers at a large universities usually have little contact and less impact on each other. In this case, however, Ralph McInerny provided guidance and moral support to this law teacher in ways of which Ralph was surely unaware.

We served together for what seemed endless years on the editorial board of the *American Journal of Jurisprudence*. When Bob Rodes and I were chosen as co-editors in 1971 (we may have been out of the room at the moment), Ralph provided throughout our service a quiet reassurance valued all the more because it came from somebody who really knew what he was talking about.

In other ways unknown to him, Ralph was sort of a lifeline for me. From my first days on campus, I was uneasy about the tension between the tradition of Notre Dame and its current commitment or lack thereof. As Bishop John M. D'Arcy said in 2009, Notre Dame has to choose between Land O'Lakes and *Ex Corde Ecclesiae*. Fr. Marvin O'Connell said in his homily at Ralph's funeral that Ralph identified with the old (and true) Notre Dame. But that "Notre Dame was gone, a fact which made Ralph uneasy because he related the change to what he saw as the diminution of the university's unequivocal commitment to the Catholic tradition. And so he became somewhat ambivalent toward the institution. Ambivalent I say—not hostile, not at all. But also, alas, not without a deep sadness." "The loyal Roman Catholic on our campuses," Ralph wrote in 1989, "no longer feels at home." To me, and surely to others, it was reassuring to see somebody of his stature who shared the same concerns we had and who voiced them so effectively. His mode was not the personal attack, and his sense of humor may have been the thing that bothered his opponents the most. His M.O. was *fortiter in re, suaviter in modo*. Ralph, however, did more than voice his concerns. He organized and supervised what became a university within the university. In his undergrad and graduate courses and in conversations in his lair at Hesburgh Library, he guided innumerable students through the maze that passes for modern philosophy to the realization that they really can know something, that there is an objective moral order rooted in both reason and faith, and that there is a God.

Ralph, I am sure, was always grateful that he was not a lawyer. He had bigger things to do. But he had a sense for the law that makes one wonder what he would have done with it. In his "Animadversions on Judge Bork," *Excelsis*, Sept. 1999, Ralph accurately summarized the Bork position: "Judge Bork believes that there is a natural law but that is none of the judge's business. . . . Thus, a judge who knows that abortion is wrong must as a judge apply the law making abortion legal—or resign. From the judge's point of view, the only relevant consideration of abortion is: legal or illegal? Moral considerations cannot enter into the discussion. . . . On the bench, a judge must be a legal positivist. It seems that there can never be an unjust law—justice being what the law says it is." Ralph carefully and precisely questioned whether insulating themselves from moral considerations is really what judges actually, and should, do. He went on to offer intriguing arguments for a practice that used to be more common among judges than it is in this positivist era: "The non-lawyer wonders why lower court judges, like dissenters on the Supreme Court, cannot weigh in with assessments of the decisions of higher courts—they might not be able to overturn them, but they could contribute to the national debate that would make clear that in a democracy fundamental decisions about the sanctity of life have been snatched from the hands of citizens by judges. It is difficult to see why chaos would result if lower court judges registered their outrage with Supreme Court decisions—this would not be to overturn them, but to acknowledge that what goes on in court rooms is not a technical exercise but a fundamental activity of the society as a whole. The judge is supposed to be justice, the virtue, personified."

Ralph was, for a philosopher, comfortably at ease in talking about legal matters. I suspect that was due to the fact that he was not wholly an academic. I know that, in a sense, he was and he was one of the best. But he had none of the insularity that is often characteristic of the breed. Academics in this era of the research university grind out "scholarly" articles and books mainly for their own advancement. And their conversation is with other academics. An apocryphal statistic has it that the average readership of a "scholarly" article is one and one-half persons; the author's spouse sometimes reads it. Ralph was more generous: In the humanities, he said, "Research is what professors do on their own, it enhances their own reputation, it is addressed to a dozen or so others interested in the same thing. The results might trickle down into classroom teaching, but this becomes increasingly doubtful." (Ralph McInerny, "The Dangers of Research," *Fellowship of Catholic Scholars Newsletter*, March 1992, 1, 2.) Ralph never fell for that idea.

Ralph was, of course, a preeminent researcher and scholar. But he was primarily a teacher. His generous attention to students at Notre Dame, grad and undergrad, was untiring and, to my knowledge, life-changing for many of them. Ralph, moreover, was not an academic snob. His mission as teacher of faith and reason, he thought, extended to all those whom he could effectively reach. His foundation, with Michael Novak, of *Crisis* magazine, which drew "venomous condemnation" from Notre Dame colleagues, was one such effort. (Ralph McInerny, *I Alone Have Escaped to Tell You*, 2006, 138–39.) So was his unique treatment of a separate Catholic topic in each thematic issue of the *Catholic Dossier* magazine he founded with Fr. Joseph Fessio, S.J. I wrote one article for *Catholic Dossier* and had the privilege of a more regular involvement in the Basics of Catholicism program which Ralph organized through the Maritain Center. It consisted of week-long seminars at which speakers in "the true spirit of Vatican II gave crash courses in the elements of Catholic culture," (*I Alone . . .*, 158). The program lasted over a decade until his wife Connie's terminal cancer forced Ralph to cancel it. To me and, I am certain, to the other participants, it was impressive to see the commitment of this genuine scholar to the task of bringing "the basics of Catholicism" to non-academic but serious persons who would put that formation to good use.

Another and remarkable accomplishment along those lines was Ralph's foundation and management of the online International Catholic University which continues to offer Master's degrees in Philosophy and Theology through Holy Apostles College and Seminary in Cromwell, CT. The initials, I.C.U., Ralph noted, "suggest the intensive care unit [and] so be it." (*I Alone*, 159.) The ICU was conceived as a critical care remedy for the terminal state of supposedly "Catholic" universities. "Why not," Ralph asked, "have a Catholic university accessible electronically, bringing the Catholic patrimony to anyone with a computer, a VCR, or an audio cassette player?" I have been privileged to offer a course on natural law in the ICU, and I can tell you that the program works and has a promising future. It is seriously and professionally administered. And it is appreciated by those who study in it.

Ralph McInerny brought multi-tasking to an Olympic level. And I have not even mentioned his novels, mysteries, etc. To me he gave edifying support for the conclusion that you don't have to be a stuffed-shirt to be an academic in any discipline, including law. I regret that I never told Ralph that he was edifying to me. His response, dismissively devastating and probably incorporating a pun, would have been worth preserving.

Charles E. Rice is Professor Emeritus of Law at the University of Notre Dame.

A Renaissance Man

When Ralph McInerny landed back in the United States and cashed his GI check, a civilian again, the first thing he did was run to a bookstore to buy a copy of *Lord Weary's Castle*, Robert Lowell's new collection of poems.

Or so he told me once, and then he laughed and gave a deprecating shrug, because—well, because that's the kind of thing smart boys with literary pretensions did in those days, and if there ever was one of those smart 1940s literary boys, it was Ralph McInerny. Besides, Lowell had produced an amazingly Catholic book, and the Catholic Renaissance that included everyone from Flannery O'Connor to Thomas Merton was about to take off in America.

They are slipping away from us one by one; the people who can remember those times that once seemed so promising. Names like Jacques Maritain and Etienne Gilson had a weight about them; you could conjure with them and see the future—a world turned high scholastic and Neo-Thomistic: Catholic philosophy and Catholic art joining to make a golden age.

On another occasion, I asked Ralph what he thought had happened—why, by the late 1960s, the whole Renaissance had faded, first to fantasy and then to dust. But he merely gave another of those shrugs and said, "We just weren't good enough."

If Ralph McInerny wasn't good enough, it's hard to imagine who could have been. He went up to Quebec to study medieval philosophy under Charles De Koninck (another in the Maritain/Gilson line, making Thomism seem, at that moment, the most exciting philosophy around). Doctorate in hand, he landed at Notre Dame in 1955—and there he stayed for the rest of his life, publishing scholarly tomes (more than fifty nonfiction volumes, in all) and establishing himself among the leading philosophers in America. *Aquinas and Analogy* is probably the most important of the books, and his Gifford Lectures, *Characters in Search of Their Author*, formed his most serious attempt to return, late in life, to the unity of philosophy and art with which he began.

He had a journalism career, as well, as a columnist and a culture warrior, founding *Crisis* magazine with Michael Novak in the 1980s. He wrote about sports, and the great moral issues of the day, and the internal struggles of the Catholic Church, and the literary legacy of his friend, the novelist J.F. Powers. He even wrote poetry, publishing a collection of Shakespearean sonnets and a volume of reflections on death.

And then there were the mysteries. Twenty-nine books starring his clerical detective, Father Dowling (played by Tom Bosley in the 1980s television series). Another thirteen set at Notre Dame. Ten more featuring a nun mystery-solver (published under the pen name "Monica Quill"), and twelve with other detectives— sixty-two mystery novels, in all, between 1977 and 2009.

It was too much, particularly when you add the nineteen non-mystery novels he also wrote (the best of them probably his 1967 academic novel *Jolly Rogerson* and his 1973 bestseller *The Priest*). Ralph had reasonably good sales and some recognition, but the mysteries to which he devoted most of his writing were always a little on the thin side—stronger in prose and character than in the actual puzzle. Besides, they had those awful titles he couldn't stop himself from giving them. As his student Thomas Hibbs remarked, the problem wasn't just that Ralph would make bad puns; it was that he seemed to prefer the bad ones—giving his books such titles as *A Handbook for Peeping Thomists, On This Rockne*, and *Nun Plussed*.

It's worth contrasting all this with Powers, the enormously celebrated Catholic writer of that same generation. When the Catholic Renaissance collapsed, Powers, undeterred, continued to write brilliantly polished, delicate prose at his same slow, one-book-a-decade rate. More of an activist, Ralph slipped instead into pour-it-out mode, never stopping to look back or revise.

He told me once that he sometimes wished he had slowed down, making a stronger effort to maintain the high literary goals of the world in which he began. But I didn't believe him. He simply lived and worked at a constant pitch of ceaseless activity.

When he died two weeks ago, at the age of 80, he took from us the last, best argument for that Thomistic synthesis of philosophy and art that had seemed so fresh and new in the 1940s. He wrote some truly fine intellectual studies and some serious fiction, but his books were a secondary effect. Really, the

Catholic Renaissance produced one of its brightest works just
by giving us the life of Ralph McInerny.

Joseph Bottum is editor of First Things.

The Seven Cardinal Virtues of
Ralph McInerny

When I agreed to say something about what's-his-name after
his funeral, I didn't expect a large audience of this magnitude. I
expected to be with the family and a few friends. I should have
known better. Ralph did not have a *few* friends. I have known
Ralph McInerny all my academic career, so I know whereof I
speak.

Ralph McInerny was a good man. On that we agree, and yet
I like to think of him under another aspect of his character,
namely, one of Plato's cardinal virtues, the virtue of justice. We
know that piety is a species of justice, the payment of a debt
where debt is due. Ralph McInerny was pious, pious toward
the source of his being, toward his ancestry, and especially
toward his deceased parents. Allow me to illustrate. The first
time I came to St. Paul at his invitation, he met me at the airport
and we immediately went to the grave site of his parents and
his three-year-old son. We then toured his old neighborhoods,
passed the homes he lived in, the school he attended, and then
to the far side of town where his piety led him to consider
the priesthood, the beautiful seminary where he studied
briefly.

A second virtue to which I call attention is his patriotism.
He loved the Ireland of his ancestry, and he loved the land to
which his family had migrated, his own country. His becoming a

Marine is only one way he exemplified that love. And we know that once a Marine, always a Marine.

The virtue of philosophy he exemplified to the fullest. He loved Plato, Aristotle, the Stoics, Aquinas, and, above all, Dante. Why, he even had a good word for Scotus. He read with appreciation and commented on their modern representatives, Chesterton, Belloc, T.S. Eliot, Christopher Dawson, and Dorothy Sayers.

His virtue as a professor was well established. As a teacher he used every means at his disposal to perpetuate the tradition that nourished him, the classroom to be sure, his professional studies, the lecture hall, his novels, and what Graham Greene called "entertainments." With Michael Novak he founded *Crisis*, he subsequently created *Catholic Dossier*, and became the editor of *The Fellowship of Catholic Scholars Quarterly*.

Entertaining was a virtue unto itself. My son, Paul, who accompanied me here, has known "Ralphy," as he was called in my family, all his life and was entertained by smoke rings and other dados as a child, long before he could appreciate the Father Dowling mystery series and other entertainments.

A sixth virtue that characterized his demeanor was his humility. Ralph McInerny was one of the most learned men I have known, but he never flaunted that learning, indulging in petty criticism or nit-picking the work of others. Why, he even accepted me as a peer.

And finally, he was kind. He would hold the step ladder for Connie whenever she decided to wallpaper, and he even bought her a ride-on mower to make her job of cutting the grass easier.

But I must tell you, he did have his flaws. Sometimes, I thought he lacked an aesthetic sense. There we were, off St. Mark's Square, watching the sun set over the west bank of the Canale della Giudecca, buildings slotted against a spectacular sky, and all he wanted to do was to drag me back to that dusty bookstore where he had previously spotted a coveted volume. The sun set without us, and in the bookstore we were punished. We did not have between us the equivalent of seven hundred dollars to buy the book. A personal check? Forget it. Plastic? The dealer was not into that. The book, if memory serves me, was an autographed Cajetan commentary on Aquinas. In the year of his death, or certainly in the year before, Ralph was still lamenting the loss of that volume.

We never encountered a bookstore we did not enter. Ralph had another habit, I can't say a fault, of succumbing to some glossy window display where we stopped to buy a trinket for Connie, as if he had something to atone for. Having traveled on four continents with him, I can assure you, he had nothing to atone for. If he didn't have St. Thomas on his mind, he had Connie on his mind.

Jude P. Dougherty is Dean Emeritus of the School of Philosophy at The Catholic University of America.

A Reminiscence of Ralph

Anyone could see at a glance that when it came time to dole out gifts to Ralph McInerny, God was feeling large. But there is more to the visibility of Ralph's gifts than God's generosity. After all, the world is full of people who squandered their endowments or buried their talents or hid their light under a bushel. Ralph's blessings were as manifest as they were because of Ralph, too. *He* recognized his God-given gifts. *He* assiduously cultivated them, and refined them. *He* exhibited them in manifold ways. Ralph's gifts were all the more conspicuous because he created such beautiful things with them. Again, the world is full of talented people pursuing self-indulgent or perverted agendas, of people who make with their gifts so many graven images. But Ralph McInerny devoted his talents to the pursuit of the truth, to understanding the Catholic faith, to serving the Church he so loved, and to providing wholesome entertainments to fiction lovers. He did all of it with unceasing love and with boundless energy.

The combined effect of all this talent and effort was often intimidating to mere mortals such as myself, endowed as we are with the usual ration of talents, and given (as we are) to spells of torpor. To his everlasting credit, Ralph had a heart for those of us on the far side of the Great Talent Divide.

I should like to share with you two of Ralph's many humane encouragements to me. One took place in the Fall of 1992, shortly after I arrived on campus. It was the 11:30 Mass at Sacred Heart Basilica, and I spied Ralph on the far side of the back pew. Afterwards, we decided to lunch. Our journey to the then legendary (now closed) Oak Room of the South Dining Hall took us across the Quad near Rockne Gymnasium. As we made our way, Ralph asked courteously how my morning had gone and what had I done. I told him that I managed a few pages of an article I was writing, that it was hard work but reasonably well done. I was content. In courtesy I returned the inquiry: "So how about your morning, Ralph? What did you do?"

"Oh, I finished two books."

Now, Ralph was already famously hard of hearing. But not so hard that he failed to hear my groan, and my gasping to recover the breath which had just exited my lungs in a whoosh. Ralph stopped and turned, and said to me very kindly: "But on one of them I didn't have much to do." He was just that sort of guy.

On that same eventful stroll, Ralph reminisced a bit himself. He recalled that twenty years before he had observed, right there by the Rockne Gym, several students running around "without their clothes on." I asked if he meant that he saw some "streakers." "Yes, yes. That was it." I knew that the first female students were admitted to Notre Dame at just about that time. So, I inquired: "Ralph, these students you saw, were they boy streakers, or were they girl streakers?" Ralph replied calmly, "I don't know. They all had bags over their heads."

The second illustration of Ralph's compassion occurred two years later in Corpus Christi, Texas. We were there for the Fellowship of Catholic Scholars' annual convention. Ralph was President; I was newly installed as Vice-President. We were invited (along with the rest of the Board of Directors) to a reception hosted by the local Ordinary, the stalwart Bishop Rene Gracida. It was all very festive with two hundred and fifty or so scholars assembled, ready for dinner and award-giving and other sources of edification.

As President, Ralph would be master of ceremonies. He had done it before to general acclaim. This time, as we glided into the banquet room he turned abruptly to me and said, "I would like you to deliver some remarks after dinner." I demurred inarticulately. Perhaps, it was my panic. Maybe it was the merlot. In any event, I knew that with his command of language and instant recall of literary, theological, and philosophical texts, Ralph could make it up as he went and still have them rolling in the aisles, laughing and crying at the same time. I would surely fall a bit short of that mark.

Ralph persisted. I explained that I had prepared nothing and had no idea what to say. He reassured me that just a few remarks would do, anything I might want to say would go over fine, and not to worry. I stammered some more. But he repeated, "I would like you to do it."

"OK, Ralph, I will."

"There is just one more thing," Ralph said, "Be very funny."

Well, I was not "very funny," probably not funny at all. I remember *trying* to be funny, at Ralph's expense. I scribbled some lines during dinner, literally on a napkin. I made Ralph's famous affection for and proficiency in Latin the foil for my remarks. The best I could do were lines like, "Ralph's newest book just came out: *Latin for Dummies.*" And like this, "Ralph is now selling cassettes as well as dime novels. He is even hawking them on TV, late night. In the commercial he promises that in six months of taped talks he can teach anyone to read *The Divine Comedy* in Latin. In a year he pledges that you'll be writing detective mysteries in the universal language of Holy Mother Church."

As I said, I would surely fall short of the mark.

"I would like you to do it." That said there was no possibility of further resistance. Not because Ralph was a bully; far from it. Not because he made it a "personal" favor. He didn't. Not because one eventually felt sorry for him and cooperated for pity sake. Not at all. He was one of the very very few people for whom asking was enough. If Ralph asked me to write for *Catholic Dossier*, I did it. If Ralph asked me to speak at his summer Basics of Catholicism course, I did that, too. If he asked for help with any one of his other projects, he got it.

And not just from me. Ralph and I just happened to be reading the same book during the last weeks of his life. It is Michael Slater's marvelous new literary biography of Dickens. From Slater, we learn that Dickens had insisted that on the masthead his role, as what we would certainly call editor-in-chief of the monthly journal *Household Words*, be called "conductor." Dickens's notion was that he made each number of the paper a unity, a harmony produced by a choir of writers.

I have myself heard many accomplished Catholic scholars explain their presence at a conference or a written contribution to a publication by saying: "Ralph asked me to." Full stop. End of explanation. This was no gang of losers. No platoon of underachievers. It was, and is, a regiment of accomplished and busy people. Their esteem for Ralph was such that his request sufficed. He was our conductor.

Over the last few years, Ralph and I explored the delights of the two-and-a-half hour luncheon. We camped regularly over at the University Club. When Notre Dame demolished that building, we moved the feast to the Morris Inn dining room. We habitually stewed over the world's problems, and those of the United States he loved so dearly, and those of Notre Dame —object by then of his mixed feelings.

During these talks, Ralph occasionally brought up his and Connie's beloved first born, Michael. Michael rests over at Cedar Grove Cemetery on Notre Dame Avenue, next to his mother and, now, his father. Michael was moved there shortly after Connie was laid to rest; he had been buried in 1957 elsewhere in town. Ralph said quite a few things about his deceased three-year-old boy. Every time he talked about Michael, he voiced his gratitude to then Notre Dame University President Fr. Hesburgh, who was extraordinarily kind to Ralph and Connie at that terrible time. But the one thing Ralph said—and it was just one time—which I shall always remember (even though I do not know why it inhabits me so), is this: "Michael was a very sick little fellow. But I never thought he was going to die until he did."

I never thought Ralph was going to die until he almost did. Ralph passed early on Friday morning, January 29. On Wednesday evening, I visited him for what proved to be the last time. I did not call ahead or check in advance with anyone. I was blessed anyway. When I got there Ralph was alone, lucid, and up for talking. I suppose I was hesitant to speak openly about what was happening, so I suggested we turn on the Notre Dame basketball. Ralph agreed. After a few minutes he asked me if I really wanted to watch the game. I said no. And we talked.

I learned then that there was no real hope for Ralph. He told me he was going into hospice, and he asked me if I "understood." Of course I did. He said that he had offered up his suffering, and I could tell that he had. At least he was visibly much more at peace than I had seen him since he learned of the cancer some ten months before. He was spiritually prepared to depart this world.

Driving home, I thought about how Ralph seemed that evening and how he was the last months. I figured out that Ralph was not and had never been afraid of *dying*. He had been afraid of *living*. He had been saddened, agitated, even mad sometimes at the thought of continuing on *without* being able to use his gifts, without his projects, without writing, without the energy and concentration even to read.

Then God smiled one more time on Ralph McInerny. God called Ralph home.

Gerard Bradley is Professor of Law at the University of Notre Dame.

Sketches of Ralph

Bruce Fingerhut, in South Bend, had kept us posted from the hospital and then the hospice. We had been stunned already two weeks earlier, when we had received the report—wrong, as it turned out—that Ralph McInerny had died. But Bruce gave us the news finally, January 29, of Ralph's death. Yet we had already experienced the sharp sense of what we were losing. As with the deaths of Richard John Neuhaus and Karen Novak over the past year, it was rather like a vast hole torn out of our lives. Most of the things we would say now could only be a filling out of Bruce Fingerhut's message to us bearing his own lament, "Ralph was outstanding in all the important roles of life: husband and father, friend and teacher, inspirer and witness, in love with God and truly loved by God. Has there ever been a happier man, a man more able to make all around him smile?"

There was the key: he was joyous, he lit up the life of friends. But as the Thomist he was, the spirit and the joy were always affected with an awareness of the things that were higher and lower, the good to be celebrated and advanced, against the lesser things, to be put in their proper place, diminished, or even cast out and shunned. There was the ever-present scale of things, with an understanding, sure and fixed, of the ends, human and divine, to which everything was rightly directed.

The first time I saw him was in a seminar in New York in 1987, when I was invited into the meeting assembled by Richard Neuhaus, at that time of course, a Lutheran pastor. As we went round the table introducing ourselves, Ralph introduced himself as "a Thomist from Notre Dame." Sitting next to him, Fr. Ernie Fortin (from Boston College) was caught by Ralph's description, and said, in a wistful haze, "I too was once a Thomist—as a teenager."

But one way or another, the writers in that room would all be involved in resisting the currents of relativism so dominant in the culture. With minor skirmishes among ourselves, we would all be involved in the project of restoring the teaching of natural law in our time, and Ralph, holding the ground of Aquinas, would always be at the center of that project. For over fifty years he would teach philosophy at Notre Dame, and he would become the director of the Jacques Maritain Center. And just a few years ago I joined him in speaking at the opening of a new project, launched by Christopher Wolfe, to form a Ralph McInerny Center for Thomistic Studies.

At a conference in Worcester in the early 1990s, I recall him taking a stringent Thomist line on assisted suicide. Death could not stand as a rival good to life, and it was at the edge of incoherence to speak of delivering a patient from pain through the expedient of simply extinguishing, not the pain, but the bearer of the pain. It was hard to see what "interests" of the person could be advanced by destroying the person himself as the bearer of those interests.

He would craft books to make the case for Thomism ever more accessible. The crowning honor came when he was asked to give the famed Gifford Lectures in Edinburgh. They were published in 2001 as *Characters in Search of Their Author*. Five years later came his delightful autobiography, with a mock dramatic title, *I Alone Have Escaped to Tell You*. But apart from his scholarly writing, he wrote also to support a growing family, and there he cultivated a whole other career as a writer of mysteries. His Father Dowling stories made it into a television series, but others came out in a steady stream of productivity— and literary craft. At one point, he had two stories at the same time in *Redbook* magazine, one under his own name and one under a female name as he shaped another series, about a nun-detective.

He called me about a year ago to tell me that he was putting Bob Royal and me in his latest mystery. I knew that I wouldn't be the one who solved the murder. Was I the one killed? No. It was a cameo, he said. A walk-on? As it turned out, not even that, and yet more. He took the occasion to take my side in an ongoing, ribbing argument within the family. He had a woman in a café in Rome point out a book called *First Things* and the man who wrote it. Years earlier, he would go into bookstores, find that book—and turn it face full on the shelf. Why would a busy writer do that? Pure friendship and pure joy.

Bruce Fingerhut told us that when he went to see Ralph at the last moments, it was Ralph who was *consoling him*. The best consolation is the hope that we may be with him one day again.

Hadley Arkes is the Ney Professor of Jurisprudence at Amherst College and this article originally appeared at thecatholicthing.org.

Like Shining from Shook Foil

He had all the virtues: wit, eloquence, pithiness, aptness, understanding, wisdom, gentility, diligence, assiduousness, courage, an iron will when it came to self-discipline, playfulness, even-temperedness, and a big appetite for hard work. Ralph had virtues for which we lack names. (What would you call the habit of never being too busy to talk—indeed positively delighting in talking—with whomever might show up at your office door—students, undergraduate and graduate, alumni, readers of your fiction, colleagues, and the just plain curious—while still accomplishing more than busy people?) Our paths first crossed in 1985 when he spoke at my graduation from Thomas Aquinas College, an institution on whose board he sat. Ralph directed the dissertations of many of its faculty, went to school with its first president, and educated its last two presidents. We next met in Washington, D.C. in the Fall of 1990 or so when I espied Ralph and Father Joe Fessio, S.J., walking in my neighborhood nearby the campus of Catholic University of America. I invited the two of them to dinner with me and my impoverished house-mates (who were, fortuitously, former students of Fessio). They graciously joined us; we enjoyed pasta and good conversation. Due to meeting Ralph that evening, I decided to attend the University of Notre Dame's graduate program in Philosophy. Upon completion of my course-work (which included Ralph's magisterial class on Aquinas' commentary on the *Metaphysics*, the *lietmotif* of which was "First Philosophy is a Theology") Ralph generously agreed to direct my dissertation, a topic about which he was skeptical (double effect), yet receptive.

As a director, he was always helpful intellectually, morally, and materially. For Ralph, helping a student was never abstract; indeed, it was very concrete: getting work back quickly, being available, never being in a rush during a conversation. Ralph had a great ability and, more importantly, willingness and desire to arrange financial support for his graduate students. I never asked for support; he simply bounteously provided it. He recalled what it was like to be a student—the pedagogical hallmark of a great teacher. The plight of the graduate student was one which Ralph never forgot, particularly that of the married graduate student with children (which I was not at the time, but which Ralph had been). Ralph proportioned the Golden Rule to grad students; we were the beneficiaries of his student-experiences. I recall Ralph's responding to a paper delivered by another Notre Dame faculty member. Ralph had a student fax the response over from the 7th floor of Hesburgh. The faculty member humorously commented on the many students to be found working for Ralph at the Maritain Center. However, the exact opposite was true: Ralph worked on behalf of and put himself at the disposal of his students. He secured funds for them, ensured they had adequate support, checked in on them, showed real interest in their work, and made himself with all his many talents immediately available to them. As his students frequently noted, he acted as if he had all the time in the world to talk to us; he accomplished so much without ever being in a rush. His example on the 7th floor of Hesburgh repeatedly comes to mind as I attempt to follow his fine example with students. Ralph's life proves the happiness of the virtuous person and the virtuousness of the happy person. For he was both, and, thus, joyous and a joy to be around. He often quoted Chesterton to the effect that real philosophers are really happy and only the mediocre ones sad. His intellectual playfulness and delight in truth lived out over an entire life is the best argument that the examined life is worth living.

I recall speaking with Ralph about how he got into writing short stories, novels, and then mysteries; a question asked of him many times, but he indulged the interested questioner, such as I was. At one point, he said that the year in which he wrote every evening from 10 p.m. to 2 a.m. was really a school of hard knocks and difficult, indeed, quite an ordeal. He bemoaned the plight of contemporary writers who have to produce a novel, not simply short stories, as he did. I was shocked. Ralph McInerny did not mention difficulties. Everything appeared to come to him with such ease. I recall thinking at the time that if Ralph found something difficult, it must have been arduous. Certainly, Ralph was natively gifted. Anyone who spent three minutes in his company immediately enjoyed his talent for and delight in language, words, and repartee. Some excellences came easily to Ralph; he was a virtuoso. It would be an error, however, to think that the ease with which he did many things was not also due to much previous hard work and past exertion.

Ralph brings to mind certain verses from Hopkins:

> The just man justices;
> Keeps grace: that keeps all his goings graces;
> Acts in God's eye what in God's eyes he is—
> Christ—for Christ plays in ten thousand places
> Lovely in limbs, and lovely in eyes not his
> To the Father through features of men's faces
>
> The World is charged with the grandeur of God.
> It will flame out, like shining from shook foil;
> It gathers to a greatness, like the ooze of oil.

In Ralph, Christ played amongst us; in him, God's grandeur gathered to a greatness: a great life, a great man. *Lux perpetua luceat ei.*

Thomas Cavanaugh is Professor of Philosophy at the University of San Francisco and the author of Double Effect Reasoning: Doing Good and Avoiding Evil *(Clarendon Press: Oxford).*

Born Writer

If anyone would want to contest the legitimacy of the category "born writer," I would, to make my case, offer Ralph McInerny as Exhibit A. Although admittedly no definitive proof can be offered to support the contention, there is ample anecdotal evidence that strongly suggests that Ralph began writing shortly after he had mastered the alphabet. By the time he was in high school, at Nazareth Hall, where he wrote for and eventually became the editor of the school's magazine, he was already in full swing. To be sure, he still had much to learn about the craft he loved so well, but his full commitment to it was by then irrevocable. I think he eventually came to look upon writing as a vocation, something to which he had been called, and, like every genuine vocation, it was something which was engaged in as much, if not more, for others as for oneself, although there is no gainsaying the fact that for him writing was pure pleasure.

In the many fine things that have already been written about him, reference is often made to the two sides of Ralph McInerny: there was Ralph the philosopher and Ralph the fictionist, the man who wrote *Being and Predication*, and the man who wrote *The Priest*. This way of looking at things is understandable enough, and up to a point justifiable, for surely one can, for practical purposes, make a convenient and suitable division of his copious writings, putting his philosophical works on one side, and his works of fiction on the other. However, I think this "two sides" approach to Ralph, if overly stressed, has a tendency to miss the fact of the essentially unified vision that guided his thought and work as a writer. If there were two sides to Ralph, they were like the two sides of a single coin, quite inseparable, and fully intelligible only in terms of one another. But that coin image has its limitations, for heads and tails are clearly opposed, and mutually exclusive, and that cannot be said of how Ralph regarded philosophy and fiction. There was always, in his writing, a constant commingling, a lively intercommunication, between the two.

In any of what can be described as Ralph's most serious philosophical writings, the voice of the novelist is frequently to be heard, but never obtrusively, never in such a way so as to distract attention away from the philosophical business at hand. Just the opposite. The novelistic inserts, if I might call them that, are always put in the service of advancing the argument. We can see this in his works on moral philosophy in particular, where examples are known sometimes to take a perky and playful form. Often before the reader is fully aware of what is going on, he finds himself caught up in the erratic antics of a mad scientist or an eccentric college professor, or he is having carefully spelled out for him certain details—illustrative of an ethical point under discussion—pertaining to the life and habits of one Fifi La Rue. As for the philosophy that is to be found in his fiction, all one needs to do for the purpose of garnering citations is to open up just about any of his novels at random and read a page or two.

As a novelist, Ralph was an unabashed moralist. He once told me that one of the reasons he had no regrets about devoting so much of his energy—which seemed inexhaustible in any event—writing mystery novels was because working in this genre allowed an author to wear his ethical commitments on his sleeve, without having to make any sly compromises or ingratiating apologies. In the mystery novel, there is no ambiguity about the real distinction between virtue and vice, and, by novel's end, virtue invariably wins out and vice gets its aesthetically and morally satisfying comeuppance. The world of the mystery novel is still a morally coherent one, where the difference between good and evil has not been blurred, or, as too often happens in modern fiction, effectively eradicated.

Ralph, as a writer, was a dedicated craftsman. He wrote rapidly, but never carelessly, just as–I like to think the comparison not too far-fetched–Mozart wrote music. He was a meticulous though not a fussy stylist, for whom language was a friendly ally to thought, and not an adversary to be battled against. In the matter of style, there is a notable difference that cannot be ignored between his philosophical writings and his fiction, and in my opinion it is in the former where he really shines. I remember stopping several years ago at a small library in Pennsylvania and browsing through its philosophy section. I pulled off the shelves a newly published volume with an inviting title but whose author I didn't know. I opened the book and discovered, not to my complete astonishment, that the Introduction was by Ralph McInerny, my relative complacency explained by the fact for this was but one of countless Introductions or Prefaces he had written over the years. Standing there in a pool of soft early spring sunlight streaming in through a nearby window, I began to read. The deeper I got into the piece, something like a delightful despair swept over me. How does he do it? It was beautifully written, the prose limpid and limber, and ambling down the page with impossible ease. The transitions from idea to idea were so smooth and inconspicuous that I had the uncanny impression that I was bearing witness to the real time weaving of a seamless literary garment. But it was not simply veneer by which I had been arrested. This was substantive philosophy, intellectual meat and potatoes, and it was being served up to the reader with commanding clarity and cogency. Within the compass of a relatively few pages, he succeeded in providing a succinct, accurate account of several thorny issues, which could only have been done by someone with the firmest grasp of his subject matter. My delightful despair (the delight coming from reading Ralph, the despair from making comparisons) was rendered all the more piquant by the sighing thought that Ralph had very likely belted out this precious piece in a single late morning sitting, before heading over to Sacred Heart Basilica for Mass, and then, later, off to lunch with a couple of colleagues.

Ralph's output as a writer, as all the world knows, was prodigious. I still stand fairly stupefied by it. But it's not just the quantity, though that's enough to make one's head spin; it is the quality that consistently accompanies the quantity. For years one of my standard one-liners was, "My brother can write books faster than I can read them." On a couple of occasions I was tempted to ask him to space his mysteries at greater intervals, just to give me the chance to catch up. I have never known—and I find this especially remarkable in light of that prodigious output of his—a more completely relaxed, utterly unflappable writer. Writing was as natural to him as breathing, and as effortless. I know he was blessed with the ability to get by with what I would consider the minimum amount of sleep—his night time slumber supplemented, however, by the daily *de rigueur* "forty winks"–but even so I do not understand where he found the time to do the reading he did, and he was a positively voracious reader, and catholic in his tastes. He kept up on everything that was worth keeping up on in philosophy, and his knowledge of literature would put many a professor of English to shame.

When I say his style shone more brilliantly in his philosophical writings than in his fiction, I do not mean to depreciate what he accomplished in the latter category. Just to cite one thing, he had few peers in the way he could manage dialogue, and it was a wonder how he deftly put it to use in establishing and developing a story line. Given his unusual skill with dialogue, I believe that, had he ever developed an interest in the drama, he could have been a noteworthy playwright. Ralph wrote poetry by way of diversion. While in Scotland delivering the Gifford Lectures, his wife Connie having at the time returned to South Bend, he whiled away his spare time writing one hundred and fifty-four sonnets, the starting point of each being the first line of a Shakespearean sonnet. The Bard gave him the cue, and he took it from there. Nothing to it. The end result, entitled *Shakespearean Variations*, is one hundred and fifty-four picture perfect sonnets, poetic gems. In response to St. Thomas's breathtaking declaration that all he had written was "so much straw," Ralph liked to quip, "Some straw!" To his poetic efforts in Scotland, and elsewhere, I say, "Some diversion!"

Last night I finished reading *Dante and the Virgin Mary*, published just days before Ralph died, and it may well be that he himself never saw the book, his last. There is no abatement in the quality of writing in this slim but poignant volume. All his talents as a writer, their luster undimmed, are fully in evidence here. The book is a fitting tribute to that great Lady and Mother for whom, in his calm and confident Catholicism, he maintained a tender and child-like devotion throughout his life, and to the great poet for whom he had boundless admiration. It is perhaps common knowledge now, at least within the family, that just a few hours before his death, Ralph, propped up in bed, asked his son for some writing materials. On the pad given him he wrote: "I commend my soul to God." It was the last thing he wrote in this world, and perhaps, of all the thousands upon thousands of words he had written over the course of his life, these were the most telling. He died early the next morning. It was January 29, the feast of Francis de Sales, the patron saint of writers.

D. Q. McInerny is the brother of Ralph McInerny, Professor of Philosophy, Our Lady of Guadalupe Seminary in Nebraska, and the author of Being Logical: A Guide to Good Thinking.

O Rare Ralph McInerny

Ralph McInerny's professional accomplishments are legendary: perhaps 125 books in philosophy, poetry, general fiction, and mysteries – plus thousands of articles and translations of dozens of books from several languages. He edited three national magazines; started an online university before they became passé; founded a book/audio publishing company producing user-friendly versions of Cliffs Notes; directed fourty-seven doctoral dissertations; headed two major centers in philosophy and medieval studies; won awards in mystery writing and, finally, philosophy's greatest award, the Gifford Lectures; all while being recognized worldwide as one of the foremost Thomist philosophers of our time.

I'll let my betters speak to such matters.

The most attractive aspect of this most attractive man was . . . the man. Ralph achieved with easy grace what every academic yearns for: to be the smartest guy in the room. But in his case, he never showed it. He always had time for students, friends, and fans. His goal was to lift people up, not put them down (remember, now, he taught at the university for fifty-five years; to be positive in such a venue is to approach sainthood). He was an outstanding teacher and writer and witness for Christ. But it was as a friend that so many will remember him. I consider him one of the closest, if not the closest, friend I have had, and I'm sure I am one of scores of people who think that. His capacity for friendship was overwhelming, lavish, effortless. His gifts of time and treasure, advice and encouragement, affability and care were all just part of being in the enormous circle of friends whom he helped and laughed with and counseled and prayed for.

He was at ease with Tolstoy and Dante, with football and movies, with Church history and Chinese food. My own mentor, Gerhart Niemeyer, once said that an educated person should be able to be say something intelligent in any conversation. He must have been thinking of Ralph, a man able to uplift the disheartened, edify the skeptic, and encourage the searcher. To be with him was to be happy.

And humor! Why, heaven itself must be shaking with laughter, now that Ralph is in their midst, bringing wit to the most mundane, and proving once and for all time that puns are the greatest form of humor.

In his final days, when I wanted to see him and wanted not to bother him, when I was self-conscious because I feared making him discomfited in his frailty, he greeted me with his usual kindness, smiling through the pain, talking enthusiastically about books and ideas and family, even though his voice was weak, putting *me* at ease, when I was there, I thought, to put *him* at ease. How fortunate are we who knew him, who know him. God is good to have put such a man in our midst.

Bruce Fingerhut is the founder and director of St. Augustine's Press, South Bend, Indiana, which has published more than a dozen books by Ralph McInerny. This contribution originally appeared on thecatholicthing.org.

The End of an Era

The passing away of Ralph McInerny, on Friday, January 29, 2010, at the age of 80, marks the end of an era in US Catholic intellectual and literary culture. He was a handsome, witty, learned and benign figure beloved by generations of students at the University of Notre Dame, America's premier Catholic university, where he taught for over 50 years. He was also a prolific author, a frequent lecturer, and a prominent public intellectual. Ralph McInerny's death was anticipated with more than personal sadness by his many friends and admirers. For with him also passed away a part of an intellectual world of literate, humane, historically informed philosophy.

McInerny was outstandingly gifted. Like many of his background and intellectual promise he was drawn to training for the Roman Catholic priesthood as offering an entry into the spheres of medieval philosophy, religion, culture and art. He attended seminaries in St. Paul, Minnesota but realized that he did not have a vocation to the priesthood and turned in the direction of professional philosophy racing through three higher degrees, including a doctorate, in the space of as many years between 1951 and 1954.

After a year at Creighton University in Omaha he was appointed in 1955 to the University of Notre Dame where he remained in post for the following fifty-four years. During that time he published very extensively within and beyond philosophy.

Surprisingly to those not already aware of the fact, his greatest output by number of books was of detective stories. These were grouped by series, most famous of which were the *Fr. Dowling Mysteries* featuring a world-wise Chicago priest and his street-wiser nun assistant. Through McInerny's invention this diocesan-duo solved thirty books' worth of crimes, from *Her Death of Cold* (1977) to *Stained Glass* (2009). The series was very successful and several books into it McInerny sold the title, character and theme to NBC who then employed the team that had scripted *Murder She Wrote* to produce over forty TV episodes.

One of McInerny's own Dowling stories was entitled *Getting a Way with Murder,* which might also have referred to his own occasional escape from the rigors of plot construction. It also hints at a fondness for punning titles, which was also indulged in his other series of detective stories as in the Andrew Broom tales (*Body and Soil, Law and Ardor*) and the series based at Notre Dame (including *The Book of Kills,* and his most recent *Sham Rock*). Such was the scale of his production of entertainments that, tiring of inventing characters, he began to introduce the names of real figures. I appeared in one of the Notre Dame "whodunits" under my own name as someone with whom a young American philosopher had come to study philosophy in St. Andrews, only later to be murdered in the competition for a tenured position back in the U.S.

Ralph's deployment of "witless" punning in the titling of his whodunits was a mark of his capacity for innocent amusement and self-deprecation that he deployed, for he was otherwise a quite masterful stylist with a deep knowledge of the literature of several European cultures as well as of modern American prose and poetry. He was also capable of great psychological and moral insight and used imaginative writing to explore the human condition as well as to provide featherweight entertainment. His 1969 book *A Narrow Time* arose from the experience of losing a three-year-old child to illness, and other novels took up the theme of moral and spiritual conflict.

It was, however, for his promise as a philosopher, historical scholar, and teacher that McInerny was employed at Notre Dame—roles he occupied with style and distinction. He held the Michael P. Grace Chair of Medieval Studies, and served as director of the Medieval Institute and Jacques Maritain Center. The appeal to him of Western Latin medieval culture was aesthetic and spiritual as well as philosophical. He read deeply in Dante and Petrarch, as well as in Aquinas and Bonaventure.

The French philosopher and public intellectual Jacques Maritain (1882–1973), though quite different in background and culture from McInerny, was a figure with whom he naturally empathized, in part because of the shared philosophical ideas, but also because of the common conviction that ideas are most extensively lived when they are embedded in cultural forms. As well as overseeing the project of producing a uniform edition of Maritain's *Collected Works*, McInerny produced an intellectual biography of the French neo-Thomist, again finding it difficult to resist word play in his choice of title: *The Very Rich Hours of Jacques Maritain* (2003). Happily he completed and published a modestly short (and wryly titled memoir) *I Alone Have Escaped to Tell You: My Life and Pastimes* (2006).

The principal focus of his intellectual work, however, was on the writings and ideas of Thomas Aquinas. McInerny produced fluid and sympathetic translations as in his massive volume *Thomas Aquinas Selected Writings* (1998). He also provided knowledgeable and insightful commentaries as of *De unitate intellectus contra Averroistas* published as *Aquinas Against the Averroists: On there being only one intellect* (1993). Beyond working to understand and evaluate Aquinas's ideas, McInerny also sought to develop them within a contemporary philosophical context.

In 1961 he published a book entitled *The Logic of Analogy* which is a detailed and technical treatment of Aquinas's account of analogical signification and of Cajetan's fallaciously derived application of this to ontology. In taking issue with Cajetan (1469–1534), McInerny was opposing himself to one of the most highly regarded and influential of the Thomistic commentators. This was done, however, with care and respect and in defense of the great truth that he believed lay within Aquinas's original writings. In a later volume, *Studies in Analogy* (1968), he gathered subsequent essays on the same subject, and in 1996 he published a fresh analysis of the whole topic, *Aquinas and Analogy,* though maintaining the original opposition to Cajetan. This book is essential reading for those interested in Aristotelian-Thomistic ideas of analogical signification and for philosophers working on general accounts of meaning, on cluster and family resemblance theories, or interested in particular applications of the idea that conditions of application of terms may vary without being altogether distinct.

Other areas in which he developed Thomistic thought were in relation to ethical theory: *Ethica Thomistica: The Moral Philosophy of Thomas Aquinas* (1982), action theory: *Aquinas on Human Action: A Theory of Practice* (1992), and natural theology: *Characters in Search of Their Author* (2001). In each case the presentation is marked by preciseness of construction and clarity of expression, qualities that made him a superb teacher and public lecturer; by wit and lack of professional aggrandizement and by a willingness to engage without fear or favor with ancient, medieval, modern and contemporary thinkers.

McInerny's facility with ancient and modern languages, and with religious and poetic as well as philosophical writings, opened him to a far greater diversity of traditions and cultures than can be found among the collective membership of a typical philosophy department. Such knowledge made him sympathetic to serious and sincere questing, but impatient of professional posturing and pouting.

His awards and distinctions were many and varied, including Fulbright grants, National Endowments for the Humanities fellowships, eight honorary degrees, membership of the Pontifical Academy of Thomas Aquinas, and of the President's Committee on the Arts and the Humanities. One of the last occasions on which I spent time with him was in the Casino Pio IV, a sixteenth century Villa in the Gardens of the Vatican. Decorated with frescoes and kept cool by thick marble walls, the villa serves as the home of the Pontifical Academies. At that point Ralph was en route back to America from an official visit to China representing the President's Committee, and he was taking the opportunity of having to break his extensive travels to spend a day or two with like-minded scholars from Europe and North America, and to refresh himself with the colour and sounds of renaissance Rome. Such was the range of his engagements.

In 1999 he was honored with a festschrift *Recovering Nature: Essays in Natural Philosophy, Ethics, and Metaphysics in Honor of Ralph McInerny* with contributions from David Burrell, Stanley Hauerwas, Alasdair MacIntyre, Alvin Plantinga, and many others including one of his six living children, Daniel McInerny, whose essay is entitled "Deliberation about Final Ends: Thomistic Considerations."

It has often been said of analytical philosophers that they focus on arguments and conceptual distinctions for their own sake without regard to historical and cultural context or existential significance. Of Continental philosophers it has been observed that they favor poetic imagination and political disposition over analysis and reasoning. Historians of philosophy are still accused of preferring to know who said what and when, rather than to evaluate the quality of the ideas or the arguments for and against them. By education, intelligence and sensibility Ralph McInerny transcended these party distinctions and managed to engage in serious philosophical argumentation, conscious of the prejudices of past and present, and directed towards the goal of determining the nature of human beings and the ends of human thought and action.

McInerny was one of the greatest figures of 20th century American Catholic culture. His brilliance emerged in his teenage years and shone undiminished for over six decades. Beyond the enormous body of his writings, his influence will continue through the very large number of his students, many of whom hold posts in US colleges and universities.

In his final weeks, conscious that his journey was nearing its end, he set aside further therapies and treatments and prepared himself for death, enjoying final meetings with family and friends and recollecting himself. His outstanding combination of intelligence, wit, and grace was rare enough, but he was also heir to traditions of broad cultured learning and aesthetic refinement that served to lift a gifted man to a quality of excellence that now seems unattainable. Those he taught whether formally or by influence and example know that he was indeed a master of masters.

John Haldane is Professor of Philosophy at the University of St. Andrews, where he also directs the Centre for Ethics, Philosophy and Public Affairs.

The Grace Professor

"Well done, good and faithful servant." No one's life can be counted in earthly words. Even Ralph who wrote so many words could not do so. His life is now recounted in the Book of Life. But here we pilgrims search for something to say as our friend has left us for now. I once called Ralph "magnanimous." But I don't think that is quite enough. I think perhaps the best word that I can think of now is "gracious." Gracious signifies the grace that filled Ralph, and the grace he shared with us. Because of his deep and abiding love of God, we can be confident that Ralph lived and died in grace. But we who were privileged to know him here, also know the ways in which that grace poured itself out as he shared his life and gifts with us—the grace of his smile, of his wit, of his writing, of his kindness.

Ralph served Our Lady's University as a faculty member for 54 years. His scholarly life began with his *Studies in Analogy* and the *The Logic of Analogy*, in which he criticized Cardinal Cajetan's interpretation of Aquinas on analogy. They nearly concluded with his *Praeambula Fidei*, in which he defends the autonomy of philosophy within the context of religious faith, and along the way returns in charity to Cajetan, now to defend him on questions of grace and nature. Ralph never held a grudge. In between are uncountable books and papers touching not only on Aquinas, but Boethius, Averroes, Newman, Kierkegaard, Pascal, Descartes, and the list goes on and on. Fifty years later, Ralph's writings on analogy in Aquinas still form the point of departure for all serious contemporary scholarship on the topic. And *Ethica Thomistica* is still recognized as the best and most accessible introduction to Aquinas's Ethics. And then there's his marvelous translation and commentary on *Aquinas Against the Averroists: On There Being Only One Intellect*. His *The Very Rich Hours of Jacques Maritain* won Christianity and Culture's Best Book in Religion for 2003. He portrayed Maritain as a saint endeavoring to live a life of sanctity in the world of ideas and politics in the tumultuous 20th century, no easy feat—it was written from the heart.

It would be folly to rehearse his scholarly CV, and even more so the novels, short stories, detective series, his little book of *Shakespearean Variations on the Sonnets,* or any of his other poetry. In one of his essays called "Mementos Never Die" (reprinted in the back of this volume), Ralph reflects upon finding prayer cards in books; the thoughts lead him on to describe the general experience of finding mementos of one's own or others in old books—a letter from his mother in a Latin edition of the *Summa,* and in his copy of Plato's *Dialogues* from 1948 the outline he had written at the age of 17 of the dialogue he would write to outdo Plato. He deadpans, "Ah youth!" Apparently that dialogue is one of the few things Ralph ever planned to write, and failed to do so. At the end of the day, he was a writer through and through, a writer of philosophy, of fiction, of poetry, of you-name-it.

In the time that Ralph served Notre Dame, he built an international reputation as a scholar of medieval philosophy, serving for several decades on the Pontifical Academy of St. Thomas Aquinas. He was president of the American Catholic Philosophical Association and received its Aquinas Medal, the American Maritain Association, and the American Metaphysical Society. He was awarded several honorary doctorates around the country. And he was awarded Notre Dame's own Faculty Award. He served in Washington on the President's Council for the Arts. And, of course, there are the awards for his fiction.

Most importantly, he was a teacher. In his 55 years, he taught thousands upon thousands of students in almost all areas of philosophy. He focused upon the work of luminaries in the Catholic intellectual tradition such as Augustine, Boethius, Aquinas, Dante, Newman and Maritain, but also others outside that tradition, such as Kierkegaard. In addition to the normal load of formal courses, Ralph was always willing to lead reading courses on Aquinas, sometimes two or three in a semester. After he ceased to offer official classes a few years ago, he continued to offer them in his home for anyone who would ask. In graduate education, Ralph is listed among the top ten philosophy professors in the United States for directing doctoral dissertations. However, that list only includes dissertations written by students in the Philosophy Department. I think he would place even higher if that list were to include the dissertations of students in the Medieval Institute who wrote on philosophical topics having to do with Aquinas. He served the department as its director of graduate studies, and directed the Medieval Institute. And for twenty-seven years as director of the Maritain Center, he provided a locale for intellectual discussion among graduate and undergraduate students alike. Despite his very busy schedule of writing, teaching, and speaking, he was always willing to drop it all and spend hours talking philosophy in his office if one had a question or two or three.

It is less well known that for the past few decades Ralph responded almost every year to the requests of undergraduates and graduate students to read informally with him classics of the Catholic intellectual tradition. Quite often these groups went on, at his suggestion, to read the documents of Vatican II as well. Among the results of this reading of the documents of Vatican II was the entry of adult converts to the Catholic faith. This is a service he provided the students here, for which he sought no recognition. It was for him simply an act of the theological virtue of charity.

Those of us who were fortunate enough to have been his students know of his tireless efforts to raise additional money to support graduate students, many of them with families, as they completed their degrees—no one who came to Ralph for help ever went away empty. Many of us would not be in the profession but for his generosity. I know of one particular instance in which he raised outside money to keep a family of four afloat, with a regular salary and benefits at Notre Dame for two years after the student had graduated. Ralph can count on the prayers of thanksgiving of all us who spent time in the Maritain Center studying in genuine leisure, not worrying about whether having more children would be a difficulty, whether we could feed and clothe our growing families, or afford health insurance for them. He has seven successful children of his own, Michael, Cathy, Mary, Anne, David, Beth, and Dan, and countless grandchildren of whom he readily bragged. But our children, his students' children, are his spiritual grandchildren, and know well of him and the life he gave us.

Finally, he weighed in on the pressing cultural and political issues of our time, founding *Crisis* magazine and *Catholic Dossier*, and writing many articles and editorials in other places. The fact, as in all things, that others might disagree with him was never a reason for Ralph not to write or express his thoughts on what mattered most to him. Perhaps Father Hesburgh captured Ralph's character best when he said of him at the festschrift in his honor a few years ago, "Ralph McInerny will always tell you what he thinks is true. I knew when I asked him for his advice that he would tell me what he thought I needed to hear, not what he thought I wanted to hear. I have not always agreed with him, but I always knew he would tell it to me straight, a virtue not often in abundant supply in the political or academic worlds. Ralph McInerny is an honest man."

While visiting Ralph recently, we began to talk about his latest project, publishing the collected works of his teacher, Charles De Koninck. Ralph said that as he worked through the papers, "I realized that I did not know what an opportunity I had back then, I wasted so much time, and did not learn enough." I was fortunate enough to be able to echo the sentiment. But if piety is appropriate on this occasion, it is perhaps best to finish with Ralph's own written words. After Connie died, and he decided to move over to Holy Cross Village, he reflected upon those events in an essay, and finished with this about Notre Dame: "My final address will be Holy Cross Village. (Penultimate, that is, my plot in Cedar Grove awaits me.) I can walk to class and my campus office. My life will be centered physically as well as spiritually in Notre Dame." He now rests with Connie and Michael, awaiting the resurrection under the loving gaze of his Mother, Our Mother, Notre Dame, in the serene knowledge that he lived a life of *veritas in caritate*, full of grace. *Requiescat in pace.*

A 1996 doctoral student of Ralph's, John O'Callaghan is Associate Professor of Philosophy and McInerny's successor as Director of the Jacques Maritain Center at the University of Notre Dame. This contribution originally appeared on thecatholicthing.org.

Remember Your Time Here

When in the spring of 2003 I told Chris Blum, a professor of mine at Christendom College, that I'd been accepted for graduate work in philosophy at Notre Dame, he congratulated me but said it was unfortunate that Ralph McInerny was not as active now as he had been. I will be forever grateful that this wasn't entirely true; that fall, my first semester at Notre Dame, he would teach a graduate course in "Twentieth Century Thomism." It turned out to be his final graduate course, but it was there that Patrick Gardner and I, his last doctoral students, made his acquaintance during his weekly smoke breaks halfway through class. (This was a few years before the ban on all smoking within 25 feet of any building, a rule that Ralph thought nicely expressed the current skewed priorities of his beloved university.)

The course was devoted to the long and friendly (though sometimes heated) debate between Jacques Maritain and Etienne Gilson about the nature of Thomism, Christian philosophy, and the role that Thomism should play in the modern world. Class always began with a prayer, either an Our Father or a Hail Mary, usually in Latin, sometimes in Greek. A few of us joined in with the Latin. He brought the course to an end with a letter written by Gilson to Father Armand Maurer in 1974 about Maritain, shortly after Maritain's death and after Gilson had read Maritain's posthumously published *Untrammeled Approaches*:

> I was naively maintaining that one cannot consider oneself a Thomist without first ascertaining the authentic meaning of St. Thomas's doctrine, which only history can do; during all that time, he was considering himself a true disciple of St. Thomas because he was *continuing* his thought. To strive to rediscover the meaning of the doctrine such as it had been in the mind of Thomas Aquinas was straight historicism. We have been talking at cross purposes all the time.

Ralph McInerny somehow managed to do both, combining historical scholarship with the firm conviction that the living Thomistic tradition was able and eager to engage, and defeat, the shifting trends of contemporary philosophy. And he inspired his students to attempt the same.

But I owe the largest debt of gratitude for my friendship with Ralph to John O'Callaghan. He arrived at Notre Dame the same year I did, and two weeks into the school year he saw me at the department's opening picnic, asked how things were going, and suggested that I stop by the Maritain Center sometime. "It's a quiet place, and I used to study up there, back when I was a graduate student," he said, "You might think about stopping by now and again." I took his advice, and by the end of the semester I had abandoned my tiny windowless carrel in favor of a desk in the corner of the Center. Ralph was still the Center's director, and he stopped by most days for meetings, to pick up mail, or to see Alice Osberger, his assistant, and by the end of that school year he had asked me to be his teaching assistant for "Dante and Aquinas," an undergraduate course he was teaching in the fall. Over the next few years, I organized directed readings with him for myself and other graduate students of Aquinas's Aristotelian commentaries (which he graciously hosted at his home across the street from Notre Dame), helped with another undergraduate course, assisted now and again with research projects, including work on *The Writings of Charles De Koninck*, and made myself generally available in the Center for all of his computer problems. (Ralph was delighted by new technology, but always thought that perhaps it might not be as easy to use as its makers consistently claimed.)

It would be impossible to convey Ralph's constant encouragement and support during my time at Notre Dame. His infectious good cheer, his sincere concern for his students' families (which often resulted in a small job here or there—to "sweeten the pot," he would say), his enthusiasm for philosophy and the intellectual life and the fledgling efforts of his students. It was also in large measure due to his help that I was able to study in Oxford for a year while I wrote my dissertation. Happily, that same year he received a fellowship from The Institute for the Psychological Sciences to spend Hilary term, from January to March, at Blackfriars in Oxford, the Dominican hall where I was writing. Though Rome was always his first love in Europe, he seemed at home as he attended the Divine Office at the Priory, Mass with the Dominicans or at the nearby Oratorian Church, and walked to a few quiet pubs where he would spend his days reading or writing. A few times he took my wife and me with our two small children out to a nearby Italian restaurant. "Remember your time here," he often said, "It will be with you for the rest of your lives." "And be grateful," he added once, telling us of his first trip to Europe as a new professor with a young family, "that you no longer have to come over by boat." The very same injunction, "remember your time here," applies to all the time I spent in Ralph's company.

Justice, thought St. Thomas Aquinas, requires that we render to others what is owed to them. But there are some debts that can never be repaid, and there are those to whom we owe what can never be fully given. For St. Thomas this most characterizes our relationship to God, the source of our very being. Though we must always give back to our Creator, we should never think that someday we will have finished. So too we must not think that we ever "fulfill our debt" to our parents, or even to our *patria*, our homeland, each of which are the source and nourishment of our existence in a more limited sense. Here we reach the limits of justice and the limits of our ability to "render what is owed." What is required isn't the repayment of the debt, the impossible equality that would come to be once we had fulfilled our obligations, but rather *pietas*. To be "pious" is to aim at rendering what is due to another, knowing that the debt can never be fully repaid, and recognizing that worship, in the case of God, and honor, in the case of men, must fill what is missing.

We most honor those who give to us of themselves by fulfilling as best we can their hopes for us, and by in turn bestowing on others what we once received. Even here I will be forever in debt to Ralph McInerny, for he will be, for the rest of my life, a model of what I will strive to become: a passionate Catholic who knew that with the Sacraments all things are possible, a man devoted to his family and to his colleagues, friends, and students, and a philosopher who strove always for Wisdom, for the solidity and joyfulness of the permanent things, and who inspired in those around him a steady confidence in the riches of the Catholic intellectual tradition. It is a great consolation that now, as he rejoices in what eye has not seen, nor ear heard, he knows too how much his life has meant to so many of us.

Raymond Hain is a Visiting Assistant Professor in the School of Philosophy at The Catholic University of America, Washington, DC. Hain's 2009 work "Practically Virtuous: Instrumental Practical Reason and the Virtues" was the last Philosophy Department dissertation directed by Ralph.

The Best of Bosses

My first acquaintance with Ralph McInerny was not with him personally but with his curious fairy tale, "The Frozen Maiden of Calpurnia," published by Juniper Press back when I was in grade school. I remember the important moral of the story, "Many are cold, but few are frozen." My second acquaintance was, also as a child, reading his book on miracles, which overcame my fifth grade intellectual skepticism about signs and wonders. Never did I dream that this Renaissance (or rather, Medieval) man would become my teacher, the person who best taught me the Catholic faith, and a wonderful boss—indeed, the last boss who has given me a $500 Christmas bonus every year just for existing. He believed in Christmas and still believed in what the world calls fairy tales or what the faithful call miracles.

As a boss, he was a great inspiration because he went to Mass every lunch but didn't make his staff go or pry into anyone's spirituality. He taught, but he didn't harangue. He believed he was witnessing a miracle at Mass and that was that. His office was fun—I think there's something about a boss who wears jeans and refuses to take himself too seriously.

Dr. McInerny really was kind without being indulgent and treated us all to the best opportunities, including repeated lunches at the University Club and Great Wall, unlimited coffee and use of the company telephone which I wore out with long distance phone calls to and from boyfriends. But everyone did that, whether it was a certain student calling some guy he needed to talk to in Rome, or the famed Latin translator Jean Oesterle calling her nieces, or other, meeker folks who would seek honest pretences to use the phone. We were all treated to Catholic conferences and fed a lot of great banquet food. It was true leisure—a vacation with a purpose—the purpose of knowing God and enjoying life. I appreciate it so much more in retrospect when I see how well everyone was treated. When Jean was too old to edit properly, we cooked up a subterfuge where she edited one set of proofs, I edited the other, and she never found out. Nobody lied there, nobody lied then, everyone really was honest because with him at the helm and Alice keeping everyone honest, there was no need, and no tolerance for, con artists. It was so important to know there was goodness in the world. (And no, Xeroxing an extra set of proofs for his benefactress, the 85 year old widow of the man who brought him to Notre Dame, is not a lie—it is a kindness. It is great respect. If you can't tell the difference between pretending and lying, please see St. Thomas's *Secunda Secundae*, question 111, art. 1, ad 1).

I think the most important things I learned from him were:

1. If you want something done, ask a busy person.
2. If something's too hard, you might not be good at it.

3. He taught me the art of effortless achievement. As a Thomist, he applied teleology to every project resulting in a rare goal-oriented form of confidence.
4. When you are around a writer, you are his material.
5. The most complicated intellectual tasks are simple, if you pray and attend daily Mass.
6. Young years are formative. Ralph McInerny was who he was because he was a minor seminarian and cared about real things since childhood.
7. Never truly embarrass anyone, ever, especially someone who is dependent on you. (To be distinguished from Irish needling.)
8. If something doesn't exist, and it should exist, you need to create it.
9. If people aren't happy, they won't accomplish anything.
10. Without a sense of humor, life is miserable, but humor makes everyone happy.
11. Take the help to lunch, give them bonuses, free books, and unlimited coffee.
12. Thomism is clear, and most other systems produce wooly-headed thinking.
13. Philosophy is not enough.
14. Don't waste your time reading everything slowly. Sometimes speed read.
15. Philosophy and Catholic learning are for everyone, and McInerny's summer camp was a great place to get up to speed on Basics of Catholicism.
16. If you're bored, stuck, or otherwise can't do your work, take a book off the shelf and start reading it.
17. The letter of Vatican II is one thing; the so-called "spirit of Vatican II" is not the Holy Spirit.
18. Someone who trusts grad students and kids to work on his books and magazines has a lot of humility and does not take himself too seriously.
19. Never walk into the office looking grumpy; he never did this once.

20. The best way to learn a language is to take the Bible and try to figure out familiar passages in the new language.
21. Last but not least, if you need to end a conversation gracefully, take out your hearing aid and start playing with it as if it is broken.

His autobiography was entitled, *I Alone Have Escaped to Tell You*. His childhood friend, Fr. Marvin O'Connell, referenced this phrase, pointing out that it comes from the Old Testament Book of Job. The devil began to try Job and take away all his family, his cattle, his possessions. At the final devastation of all Job's possessions, but one witness would escape, recount the story to Job, and say, "I alone have escaped to tell you"(Job 1:15). Ralph McInerny inhabited a bygone world, but he alone escaped to tell us. He told us the truth of Catholic philosophy and theology, and he taught us with his example and classy leadership and kindness. Someday, as in the story of Job, this patrimony and this world of Christian gentility will be restored twofold. Miracles still happen. Ralph McInerny, rest in peace, until that day.

Ellen Rice is currently a publishing freelancer and the editor of The John Paul II Life Guide: Words to Live By. *She has developed curriculum for the Catholic Schools Textbook Project and St. Augustine's Press. In her spare time, she is gradually pursuing a Master's in Theology from Holy Apostles College and Seminary, through a distance education program developed by Dr. McInerny and the International Catholic University.*

Letter of Appreciation

To the members of the Ralph McInerny Family, to his many colleagues, students, friends assembled at Notre Dame, and other dear friends from around the world.

I extend my deep condolences and assure you that I share your profound sorrow, a sorrow made more profound because I am far away and cannot bring you whatever little consolation might be given by my presence.

What can one say about dear Ralph McInerny that might be adequate? His extraordinary life of study, teaching, prayer, and his devotion to his family, especially his beloved spouse, Connie, whom he loved with his whole heart, remain an example for us all. His writing so varied, rich, lucid, and always Catholic to the core, will still teach us in the years ahead. He was a mentor to young philosophers, a teacher to generations, a man of genuine holiness, a truly Catholic philosopher, a student of the great Thomas Aquinas, and a man for whom there was no division between the intellectual life and the spiritual life. His love for the Church and his fidelity to it marked his years and continue to inspire us.

I will always remember his joyfulness. While sometimes troubled by what he observed in the Church and in the surrounding culture, it never diminished his steadfast love and hope. Even with the terrible loss of his beloved Connie, he carried on—though with great and obvious pain—strengthened by his children and grandchildren, with the knowledge that she had indeed lived a full and worthy life. We have every reason to hope and believe that he now shares the vision of God, about which he wrote, relying on the teachings of his beloved Thomas Aquinas. As followers of Jesus Christ, Catholic and others, let us take consolation in this hope.

I think it appropriate to conclude these remarks with some words I was privileged to recite year after year at the conclusion of the Notre Dame Baccalaureate Mass. They are from another great philosopher: Pope John Paul II: "Faith and reason are like two wings on which the human spirit rises to the contemplation of truth; and God has placed in the human heart a desire to know the truth—in a word, to know himself—so that, by knowing and loving God, men and women may also come to the fullness of truth about themselves" (*Fides et Ratio*).

I shall offer Mass for Ralph and the McInerny family.

Sincerely yours in our Lord,

Most Reverend John M. D'Arcy

Bishop Emeritus, Diocese of Fort Wayne-South Bend

This letter from Bishop D'Arcy of the Diocese of Fort Wayne-South Bend was read aloud at Ralph's funeral reception.

His Last Course, His Last Graduation

I was blessed to be present for and involved with the conclusion of his astoundingly long career as a professor at Notre Dame. Before and after his death, many have already remarked on the devotion he showed in teaching at the university for more than 50 years, and I have a particularly and personally keen appreciation for that devotion. It was only by grace of this tireless love for Notre Dame and for his vocation that I was able to work with him in those latter days. He could easily have retired, decked with well-earned laurels, before I entered high school!

I was privileged to be his Teaching Assistant for his last (official) course, "Dante and Aquinas." Two aspects of the class stand out in my memory.

The first was how his lectures exemplified the characteristics which always marked his scholarship. He combined his own rigorous textual analysis and comprehensive knowledge of scholarly debates (necessary for an academic, of course, but often conducive to deadly dullness) with a perfectly lucid and even casual presentation which was no less engaging to the neophyte.

This was not just a product of his lecturing style and his wit, of course (though these were inimitable), but derived especially from the material, i.e., from the ideas he wanted to teach. It is one thing to dumb down a theory, or to present merely a sketch or outline of it, it is another to be utterly convinced that the high-level scholarly debates have in fact gone astray—lost in a *selva oscura* of technical terminology taken for granted which conceals the truly pressing and human concerns at issue—and that the introductory reading of a great text is where the battle is really to be fought.

The class covered a huge amount of material, supposedly at the beginner's level, and allowed me finally to begin to understand Aristotle seriously and deeply, especially with regard to the *Physics*. Ralph used nothing of the technical terminology (of hylomorphism, causation, etc.) which I knew off-handedly and superficially, but presented the Parmenidean problem as a living and serious challenge, not so much to our common-sense realism as to the relationship between that realism and our philosophical speculation, and thereby got more into the mind of Aristotle than the most learned post-Jaegerian classicist.

On the last day of the course when he had finished the very last classroom lecture he was to give at Notre Dame after 50-plus years, I had it in mind to mention the occasion to the students and invite a modest appreciation. But when I made a motion in my seat and cleared my throat, he looked over, and then turned back to the class and asked them to give *me* a hand, for deigning to grace the course with my presence. When after a moment I had recovered, he was already on his way out the door. I felt terrible and quickly arranged a later gathering for the class, to atone for my mistake and to celebrate his achievement. Only afterward did I realize how effortlessly he had saved me from my own awkwardness, and how he had ended his final lecture on one more, very wry, joke.

Last May, even though he was already suffering mightily from what would turn out to be cancer of the esophagus, he was kind enough to walk with me at graduation to receive my doctorate (the Graduate School's ceremony was entirely separate from the all-school Obama-fest the following day, which neither of us had any intention of attending). We were sitting through a terribly boring speaker, and I was trying very hard to maintain a solemn and attentive visage appropriate for the occasion, to think of myself as taking part in a grand medieval tradition, entering into an elect and austere company, made especially present by Ralph's extravagant Laval gown at my side. At one point, I glanced to see Ralph, fur collar and all, leaning over his iPhone, like any bored undergraduate texting during class. (He was looking at pictures of his family.) Perhaps, he had one last lesson for me, not to take oneself too seriously.

Patrick Gardner's 2009 work "Dante and the Suffering Soul" was the last Medieval Institute dissertation directed by Ralph.

A Guardian Angel

I am very grateful for the fatherly way in which Ralph shepherded me through graduate school. He was a very busy man and yet if I ever wanted to see him he would open his door. Sometimes it seemed that his colleagues had a significantly harder time getting past Alice than did we powerless students.

Ralph started looking out for me before I arrived at Notre Dame, indeed before I had ever met him. I applied for the Medieval Institute and was accepted with tuition but no money. Jude Dougherty at The Catholic University offered tuition and promised to arrange money. The choice seemed clear but I wanted to talk it over with my brother, who was already in South Bend. He had a simple answer. "I'll ask Dr. McInerny." The next day he called back. "Dr. McInerny says to come here . . . we'll work something out."

And he did "work something out." The upshot was that I wound up with a Bradley Fellowship and the injunction to spend time in the Maritain Center. There were things to do, and he was glad for the help. Mostly he wanted us to have a friendly place to be, a place characterized by lively conversations of all sorts. I remember filing DeKoninck papers and arguing about the principles of self-defense, and the precise definition of a lie with Steve Jensen, John O'Callaghan, and Mike Letteney. We had a wonderful graduate student seminar one day upon the release of John Paul II's *Veritatis Splendor*, with about 20 students from various departments. Jean Oesterle would stop in and chat. And Alice oversaw all of it and made sure we didn't get too abstract for our own good. I am very grateful to Ralph for putting me in a strong and friendly intellectual environment.

I remember Ralph coming out of his office, the inner sanctum, and taking a few practice golf swings. "I just finished writing a letter of recommendation for one of my students." Long pause. Another swing. "I feel like I should go to confession now."

He could get very defensive about his students. I know that I wouldn't have graduated if it weren't for him. He put them and their welfare first. I remember strongly urging one of my fellows, Christopher Kaczor, to abandon his foolish plan of writing under a distinctively non-McInerny type. After much earnest cajoling he did, in fact, ask Ralph to be his director. Almost twenty years later, he still thanks me for this every time I see him.

Ralph was especially attentive to young families. When graduate school was dragging on a bit, and baby number two had arrived, my wife, Karen, broke it to me that we needed more money. She convinced me that we should take out a loan from the government. I hated to do that because the credit card debt was already mounting, but if we needed it, we needed it. Embarrassed, we told no one. So I asked her to give me an amount and I would file the papers. When she gave me the figure I went to campus with plans to work a few hours at the Maritain Center and then go to the Administration Building after lunch to file the papers for the loan. Shortly after I got to the Maritain Center, Alice said that Dr. McInerny wanted to see me.

In his office, he explained that I had been with him several years and that he was mindful of the new addition to my family. In short, he wanted to raise the amount of my fellowship to help me through my final year. When he told me how much, my jaw fell. It was the exact amount that Karen had mentioned, the exact amount I had listed on the loan papers. Karen and I had not spoken of our intention to anyone. Whether or not it was divine inspiration, it is still remarkable that he was so solicitous for his student's well-being that he could see the need without being asked.

Brian Kelly is Dean of Thomas Aquinas College in Santa Paula, California.

He Had Our Number

I am a fairly undisciplined and compulsive reader, but I sometimes think the number of books Notre Dame's Ralph McInerny has written exceeds the number of books I have read. Along with the countless volumes of philosophy, literary criticism, cultural criticism, and poetry that the late Michael P. Grace Professor of Medieval Studies left behind when he died on January 29, are dozens of potboilers, many of them murder mysteries.

My favorites among this subset of "McInernia" are the novels Ralph set at Notre Dame. All of them have groan-inducing puns in their titles, such as *On This Rockne, Irish Tenure, Lack of the Irish, Celt and Pepper,* and the forthcoming *Sham Rock.* (When it came to resisting puns, Ralph was utterly powerless. He once unblushingly began a lecture on G.K. Chesterton this way: "It takes a lot of gall to talk on Chesterton, and my gall is divided into three parts. . . .")

Ralph's Notre Dame murder mysteries are lavish in local color and character, and he often included thinly disguised friends and colleagues as minor characters. I was always delighted and amused by the good-natured teasing involved in these cameos until, in a couple of the stories, I noticed a character from Notre Dame's PR office with a name suspiciously like my own.

"All this guy does is hang out in the back bar of the University Club, drinking, telling cynical jokes and picking fights," I grumbled to my wife. She replied that she could fondly remember several times we had sat with Ralph in that very room, drinking merlot, joking and gossiping about the peculiarities, splendid and otherwise, of Notre Dame. She gently added that if I didn't exactly pick fights on those occasions, I did from time to time express vehement and contrary opinions. "In other words," she shrugged, "Ralph's got your number."

She was right, of course. Nor was mine the only number this incisively witty and wonderfully convivial man had, which is among the reasons he could be such a formidable controversialist. Whether his aforementioned gall was divided or not, he had gall aplenty, and he could be positively gleeful in flushing out, strafing and demolishing an opposing viewpoint, especially if that viewpoint concerned the affairs of the Catholic Church.

But if he spoke and wrote daggers, he used none. Too honest to shrink from genuine disagreement, Ralph also was too kind to keep an enemy. "I have never doubted the sincerity of those I have called dissenting theologians," he wrote in his autobiography. "Many of them are friends of mine."

Among those sincere believers with whom Ralph could vigorously disagree were many men and women of the Catholic Worker movement. But any of them will tell you they had no better friend than Ralph McInerny.

During the years since Ralph's retirement, Notre Dame theologian Michael Baxter, an active member of the Catholic Worker community in South Bend (and a minor character in one of Ralph's Notre Dame mysteries), was a frequent and welcome visitor at Ralph's house in Holy Cross Village. They liked to talk about theology and Catholic history, but Ralph would often ask after the affairs of the Catholic Worker houses. Not only the plights and idiosyncrasies of the guests would interest him, but also the grocery, heating and repair bills. Often Ralph would nonchalantly remark, "I can help with that," scrawl an eye-popping sum on a personal check, and hand it to Baxter, never letting his right hand know what his left hand was doing.

Charity was perhaps the only activity in which this eminently meticulous philosopher could be so careless.

Michael Garvey is Notre Dame's assistant director of public information and communication. This article first appeared at http://magazine. nd.edu/.

Encounters with Ralph McInerny

I first saw Ralph in action at a meeting of the American Catholic Philosophical Association in Detroit in the Spring of 1958. I was myself at the time a graduate student teaching a course at St. Michael's College, University of Toronto, and thinking that I might have to get a full-time job, though I had not finished my doctorate. Who was this brash young speaker criticizing my teacher and thesis director, Etienne Gilson? However, I had no opportunity to speak with him.

My next conscious encounter with him (also at an ACPA meeting) was in his capacity as editor of the *New Scholasticism*, the ACPA periodical, when I told him that I had a lengthy article criticizing Fr. Owens's conception of existence. He was eager to see it and eventually published it (published in 1982, thus much later than my first mentioned meeting).

I know I was very much pleased when Ralph congratulated me warmly on my presidential address to the ACPA, "Truth and Happiness," March of 1993 in St. Louis, Mo. Here was praise worth having!

I remember (again, I believe, at an ACPA meeting) inviting Ralph to speak to the Canadian Maritain Association at a meeting in Calgary, Alberta in the summer of 1994. The general theme was to be "theories of the history of philosophy," and Ralph spoke on Kierkegaard. To quote a report I wrote at the time: "He gave a remarkable paper on Kierkegaard, Hegel, and the relation between ethics and historically significant action."

Closer friendship with Ralph arose from his invitations to take part in the Summer Thomistic Institutes (which I did on at least three occasions). What a wonderful initiative they were! And how much the organization of them testified to Ralph's Catholicism! What with the liturgical prayers at the talks, and the Masses (in the Charles Borromeo Chapel, as I recollect), it was all most edifying. And the group in attendance testified to the breadth of Ralph's acquaintance. Both he and I subsequently took part in a colloquium at Fu Jen University in Taipei (and we both eventually gave lecture series there), thanks to invitations from Ursuline Sisters Marian and Pascal, whom I met at one of the Summer Institutes. Another Institute bonus was Bill Carroll's urging everyone to take advantage of the Templeton Foundation largesse for presentations on science and religion. I keep a photo of the members of the 2001 Institute, taken in front of the Notre Dame Law School, very prominent in my room (and am very proud to be seated next to Ralph).

As an avid reader of detective fiction, I have enjoyed many of Ralph's books, whether about Notre Dame or other of the various settings.

Philosophically, of course, we are both Thomists, and some of the things I did pleased Ralph, such as my criticisms of Etienne Gilson and Fr. Owens. However, we also had our differences, particularly as regards whether one needs first to prove the existence of the incorporeal in order to bring metaphysics into existence. Unlike me, Ralph espoused "the River Forest position," that one does so need.

Until the last five years or so, I had not participated regularly in the activities of the American Maritain Association (I was one of the founding members of the Canadian Maritain Association, and served it over the years in various ways). In 2005 John

Hittinger invited me to speak at the Washington meeting in the fall on metaphysical renewal. That prompted me to continue participating, and in November 2006 I spoke at Nashville.

On that occasion, much to my surprise and delight, I was presented with the Association Medal for Scholarly Excellence, and by Ralph himself! However, Ralph introduced me as (like himself) a graduate of Laval University! I take this as a compliment. However, as I stressed at the time, I am as thoroughly a product of "Toronto Thomism," let us say, as one can be. I attended St. Michael's College as an undergraduate, and subsequently did my graduate studies on the Toronto campus (including the Pontifical Institute of Mediaeval Studies). I revered both Charles De Koninck of Laval, and Gilson (and Maritain) of Toronto, and still do so. And I began my philosophical publishing with an article in *Laval théologique et philosophique* in 1971.

I last really socialized with Ralph in February of 2008 at Blackfriars in Oxford. I was there from the 18th to the 24th; I lectured on the 20th and the 21^{st,} Wednesday and Thursday, and Ralph came to both. I had not known that he would be on hand, and my seminar presentation was on "First Known Being and the Birth of Metaphysics," very much at odds with Ralph's views. (I took some pleasure, I'm afraid, in reminding him that Maritain held that philosophy of nature participates in metaphysics; I can still hear Ralph's exasperated "I know he did!")

In fact, that is what I have admired in Ralph and our many mutual friends, that we all have in view "*magis amica veritas*," i.e. that the truth is what counts, and we must work to find it; and, as Aristotle says, we have debts to those with whom we disagree.

On my last evening there, when I went to a pub with Bill Carroll, Ralph just happened to be there watching the young student life go on. (Ralph had given one of the Blackfriars seminars the month before, Jan. 24, on "ordinary knowledge of God.") And so we had a good visit.

I did see him subsequently in June of 2008 at the Vatican, for the meeting of the Pontifical Academy of St. Thomas Aquinas, but, as it happened, had not much of a chance to talk with him. Nevertheless I heard him read his paper: "Newman and Natural

Religion: *ex umbris et imaginibus.*" He was even then joking about our mortality with a pun; and I quote:

> In what follows, I attempt a sketch of what we can learn from Cardinal Newman on the matter of the *praeambula fidei*, a sketch whose inadequacy I need not stress. Much of what I allude to here requires a much fuller treatment, one I hope to live long enough to undertake. But if the undertaker wins the race, I will be happy to have made even this poor contribution to the appreciation of the thought of John Henry Newman.

In 2008 I published a review of Ralph's book, *Praeambula fidei: Thomism and the God of the Philosophers*. He tells us in this book's preface that he means "to treat the negative attitude towards natural theology that is found among those one would have expected to be defenders of it." [p. ix] He says, "This book is a defense of a robust understanding of the teaching of St. Thomas Aquinas and of the Magisterium on *praeambula fidei*" [p. ix]. This, I would say, is an essential task. It required that one criticize some of our own most distinguished teachers. Ralph did not "soft-pedal" in this regard, but neither did he forget to remind us of what we owed to those same teachers.

Ralph was a "public philosopher" and he presented his views with courage and aplomb. As with Jacques Maritain, a festschrift for him could well be called "*Un philosophe dans la cité/A Philosopher in the World.*"

Lawrence Dewan, O.P., is Professor of Philosophy at Dominican University College, Ottawa and is the author of Wisdom, Law, and Virtue: Essays in Thomistic Ethics, Form and Being: Studies in Thomistic Metaphysics, *and* St. Thomas and Form as Something Divine in Things.

A Letter to My Benefactor

14 June, 2009, Feast of Corpus Christi
Dear Ralph,

I want to express my gratitude to you. The "thank you" is not only for your work and life in general, but also and specifically, for your effect on my husband Rollin and me. How can I explain just how important you have been to us and to so many others?

When the academy, culture, and established religion began its implosion in the late 1960s, we were newly weds and parents of young children. After Rollin's promising career launch in the mid1960s and a splendid beginning in 1967 to our married life in the Anglo-Catholic tradition, our life began to disintegrate with the times, "they were a-changin'." We began to feel very alien in our own culture and families by 1970.

When we came to Notre Dame in 1975 for Rollin to take a post-doc in the liturgy program, it was beyond insane—with balloon liturgies and "Feeling Groovey" as the entrance song at Sacred Heart. We heard people talking about you, as you were already well-known for doing what you do so well: defending the Truth and teaching the Faith, in season and out. Rollin wanted to meet you, but he felt inadequate and ashamed to make the connection because he felt that he had failed; he had left the secular university position and was unsure of his religious home, being neither fish nor fowl.

Throughout those years leading up to and after we moved to South Bend, we had been inspired by your wit and energy – and we subscribed to *Crisis* as charter readers; it was a beacon to us, then, as *Catholic Dossier* was later. We always took heart from your example of courage, clarity, generosity, and loyalty. In particular, I know how much Rollin envied and appreciated your philosophical intelligence; it was a training that he did not have. In so many ways, we applauded and were inspired by your heroic actions at Notre Dame; often, your embattled position appeared to be like "Athanasius against the World."

It was the "Basics of Catholicism" that was one of the most influential events of my adult life. Rollin and I both felt like we had our compass and map back in our hands, again! We had become Catholic in 1980, after a very painful severance from our Anglican heritage. I learned church history, doctrine, morality, and current political issues, which have influenced me to the present.

Based on your advice, Rollin and I settled on the University of Dallas as a college for our children. All but our oldest son graduated from UD and all have become teachers at various universities and schools around the country. So, indirectly, you gave our children their launching pad for their teaching careers, too.

Of course, not all of your influence in our lives has been of a serious nature. As we traveled back and forth the many times that we made the trip between Indiana and Texas, we read your book, *The Search Committee*, and we laughed our eyes out!

We have been happy and honored to know you, to have been guided by you, to have been able to break bread with you. May the blessing that you've given to us return to you! In the Communion of Saints, we all are friends, in the bonds of Love.

You are at the front ranks of the truly great teachers, and so I send it along as a tribute to you, too – husband, father, professor, philosopher, scholar, poet, writer, and defender of the faith. Thank you, dear Ralph!

With continuous prayers, gratitude, and love.

Ruth Lasseter is a mother and wife.

The Designated Hittinger Shows Some Leg

In the fall of 1972, I sat in a classroom under the golden dome; a newly declared philosophy major, I looked forward to a class on ancient and medieval philosophy. Ralph McInerny strode in and sat in front of the professor's desk. That calm earnestness about the task of philosophy combined with a joyous wit characterized his presence in that first encounter and such a presence marks my memories of him over numerous years of association. The next year I took another class from him on the thought of Aquinas, which later became the book, *A First Glance at St. Thomas Aquinas: A Handbook for Peeping Thomists.* Combining the exposition of texts, historical context, clear thinking, logical arrangement, homespun examples, with the goal of wisdom always in view–Ralph was the consummate teacher. With more than thirty years of teaching experience, I can say that I still aspire to be like him in the classroom. Devotion to Thomas Aquinas and Catholic faith were a natural part of his persona and repertoire. It was during the semester that I was enrolled in the Aquinas class (Spring 1974) that he was named to the Pontifical Academy of Thomas Aquinas. I remember the pride he took in the appointment, and the joy with which he planned his trip to Rome. I approached him after one class prior to his trip and expressed my disappointment that he would be absent from class for over a week. He looked me in the eye and assured me that students in Europe did not need such hand-holding, "Go read your Thomas." I took the opportunity to read his *Thomism in an Age of Renewal* and began to get some glimmer of the battles that he undertook for the wholeness of truth and the authentic renewal of the Church. Earnest and witty, learned and spirited, McInerny made the case for Thomas and the Catholic tradition with aplomb. He would later write *What Went Wrong with Vatican II* in the same style. I cannot think of two better books for understanding the role of the Catholic intellectual after Vatican II. In addition, he launched *Crisis* magazine (for which he asked me to serve as a writer and board member) and *Catholic Dossier*. He organized Thomistic Summer Institutes and Basics of Catholicism workshops; I attended a number of the Summer Institutes. We felt like a clan, a tribe of Thomists, blessed by good fortune to have such an illustrious chief in the likes of Ralph McInerny. The fight was always confident and joyful, not bitter; the weeklong meetings were both pious and rollicking; and he presided over some marvelous intellectual conversations and debate, many of which are available still on line and in books on Augustine Press. And the circle spread out far and wide—Neuhaus seminars, Liberty Fund, American Maritain Association, Fellowship of Catholic Scholars, American Catholic Philosophical Association—Ralph was a constant and engaging participant, always a friendly face, and eminently a witty conversationalist.

Not only the scholar and teacher, the spokesman and chief— Ralph was a personal mentor for many young Thomists, including myself and my brother Russ. We always felt that he took a personal concern for our lives, families, and careers. We shared a love for the Church, the Marine Corps (our father was career Marine who died in Vietnam), and Thomistic philosophy. My brother and I would often be invited to the various events mentioned above, and on different occasions one or the other of us could not attend. Quick on the draw, Ralph quipped at a Neuhaus seminar that I was "the designated Hittinger" for that day, a phrase he would always use thereafter whenever one of us was not in attendance. He would often have some affectionate play on words for many of the young scholars—I remember once at a conference Ralph and I were at the table with Father Canavan and Regis Factor, a professor at the University of South Florida, who died of ALS in 1999; Regis was conveying to us some discouragement he was facing at his institution and Ralph banged the table and exclaimed, "But they have underestimated the 'Regis Factor.'" Regis was perhaps an overly serious young man, so Ralph said it a few more times and at last Regis quietly smiled and beamed with the encouragement.

My own professional career owes much to Ralph's personal intervention. My first conference presentation was delivered at Notre Dame for the American Maritain Association concurrent session at the annual meeting in 1983 because Ralph proposed my name to the program chair, Sister Mary Clark. I prepared by reading and annotating everything written by Maritain on political philosophy. "A Prologomena to Any Future Critique of 'Bourgeois Liberalism,'" I entitled my paper. Ralph sat in the front row. He shook my hand afterward and encouraged me to publish it—it appeared in *This World* along side a piece by

Allan Bloom. Ralph's advice to me as a young scholar was to get around and show your stuff, "show them some leg," he said. Ralph was truly a man in the world, but not of the world. I still relish that piece of advice for its wit and wisdom.

In 1990, I was teaching at the College of St. Francis in Joliet, Illinois. That year my wife, Molly, and I welcomed our third child. With three children under four years old, full teaching and administrative duties, the time for research and writing was scarce. I drove to South Bend and visited Ralph in the Maritain Center. Ralph and I concocted a scheme for arranging a post-doc fellowship at Notre Dame which would involve a course load reduction through a payment for adjuncts. I am not quite sure how it all worked out, but the Fellowship appointment and the letter from McInerny was as good as gold with my Dean. Once a week I would drive to South Bend early in the morning and spend the night with a friend like Phil Sutton (a fellow undergrad philosophy major who recommended to me that first course with Ralph) and then return the following evening. Ralph, Alice Osberger and the grad students at the Center were hospitable to my efforts to read and write. One afternoon, I was standing with Ralph in his office on the seventh floor of the library. From his window one could survey the grand expanse of campus, especially the dome glinting in the sun. He was rightfully proud of the office and the view. I looked below to see Breen-Phillips Hall, my residence hall for two years. Not yet forty years old, I began to speak nostalgically about arriving on campus twenty years ago on a Greyhound bus from Alexandria, Virginia. Ralph, who was sixty-one, spoke about his arrival on campus thirty-five years ago. *Sic transit Gloria mundi*, yes, but how glorious it was and how grand the alma mater.

We repeated the arrangement for a second year. His encouragement continued. He invited me to give two courses for the International Catholic University, one on modern philosophy and another on political philosophy. During his last year he called me and spoke about "the lengthening of the shadows" and his desire to get various projects squared away. He asked me to serve on the board for the ICU, and he was enthusiastic about its prospects for the future. He expressed hopes that the University of St. Thomas, Houston, would be able to do something in partnership. I look forward to working with Dan McInerny in keeping this important project on track. Ralph had also agreed to let me form a team to translate the first book by Maritain, *Antimoderne*. Working in fits and starts over many years with my colleague Rich Lemp, a French professor at the U.S. Air Force Academy, we are very close to completing this project.

In this last decade I continued to work with Ralph on various other projects. I served as vice-president while he was president of the American Maritain Association. We held some terrific conferences on the Vocation of Philosophy (the papers from this conference are soon to be published) and on the Philosophy of Nature. Perhaps the proudest moment of my association with Ralph McInerny was at one of these Maritain conferences. A special meeting brought me together with Ralph and John McGreevy, now dean at Notre Dame, for a "meet the author" session. My book under consideration was *Liberty, Wisdom and Grace* and Ralph's was *The Very Rich Hours of Jacques Maritain*, and McGreevy's was *Catholicism and American Freedom*. Ralph's book is perhaps his best of all on the vocation of Catholic philosophy; add it to the list of essential reading for appreciating the McInerny legacy. I am also proud my the connection with Ralph and Jude Dougherty, by being considered along with them in an article by Nicholas Capaldi, "Jacques Maritain: La Vie Intellectualle," published in 2004 in the *Review of Metaphysics* (58(2): 399–421).

The life, the work, and the friendship of Ralph McInerny have framed a deep symmetry in my life and my connection to the University of Notre Dame. Forty years ago, in the fall of 1970, I arrived on the campus of the University. I was a teen-aged refugee from the steties, distracted by the counter-culture, confused by the changes in the Church and in the country. Through contact with Ralph McInerny, Joseph Evans, and Frank O'Malley, I was blessed to encounter the Catholic intellectual tradition in an imaginative and persuasive form. With joy I have read Maritain, Guardini, Simon, Pieper, Dawson, Gilson, and Newman. With a deep calm, confidence, and joy did they face the crisis of our time—the erosion of truth, the marring of man, the violence of wars, and the loss of liberty. And they propounded the integral humanism of Aquinas and Augustine, which now is the integral humanism of Paul VI, John Paul II, and Benedict XVI. Against the secular trends in society and academia at large and the liberal Catholicism emerging at Notre Dame, McInerny, Evans, and O'Malley pulled us in to the Catholic counter-culture. Twenty years later, in 1990, McInerny remained, and he continued to pull them in and send them forth. And now in 2010, a second score hence, I returned to South Bend for his funeral. Ralph McInerny was, for me, the best hope of Notre Dame. With a full-throated ease, he witnessed to the beauty of the Catholic mind and Catholic culture. He now joins Evans and O'Malley in a golden glory, brighter than the dome. The memory of them will long outshine the tarnish of the institution and their songs will be sung high above the compromised mutterings of the clerks who now roam below that seventh floor perch of the Maritain Center.

John P. Hittinger is Professor of Philosophy at University of St. Thomas, Houston, TX.

To Miss the Joy Is to Miss All

I first met Ralph in the summer of 1953, at our family home in Quebec City. He was then studying for the doctorate at Laval University, and was putting order into my father's papers. This had been a ruse to help him financially, as he narrates in his splendid memoir, *I Alone Have Escaped to Tell You*. I was 19, and he was 24. We had long conversations on literature, where he would introduce me to contemporary American and English poets I did not know, and I rather stuck to Shakespeare. His acumen and elegance of expression were remarkable even then.

His phenomenal wit and wonderful sense of humour were discoveries I made later.

I followed from afar his doctoral dissertation on Kierkegaard, which he wrote under the direction of my father, Charles De Koninck, who spoke very highly of it. Everyone interested in Ralph's thought should read his article emanating from it, *A Note on the Kierkegaardian Either/Or* (in *Laval théologique et philosophique*, vol. VIII, no. 2, 1952, p. 230–242). My father told me more than once that Ralph had been his best pupil.

It is, however, as a colleague at the University of Notre Dame, where I taught philosophy from1960 to 1964, that I had the great fortune to come to know him better. I have nothing but fond memories of those four years at Notre Dame, where I initially shared an office at O'Shaughnessy Hall with John Oesterle, Joe Bobik, Ralph, and others. I can still see and hear, as if it were yesterday, Ralph taunting me in that office for not having read novels of his which lay hidden, so far as I could tell, in a drawer somewhere. This must be what he calls, in his memoir, "those dubious novels of yore" (63).

We soon became close friends. One recurring concern in our discussions was the teaching of philosophy in a Catholic university, with at its core the all important question of the relation between faith and reason, which the beloved Pope John Paul II was to underscore later so strongly. *Philosophandum in fide* was a principle Ralph held at heart. He deplored the fact that it was not respected as it should be, even at Notre Dame. I remember vividly a courageous lecture he gave in the early sixties on the topic, before colleagues, for which he was much taken to task, answering with a lucidity I have seldom witnessed in such debates since. This involved as well the crisis of confidence in the powers of reason which makes much contemporary philosophy abandon the study of the ultimate questions, as his memoir makes crystal clear in the chapter aptly entitled, "Learning How to Die."

The ultimate question *par excellence* is, of course, the question of God. It was predominant in our minds even then and eventually gave birth to books. On 2 July 2003, he wrote me, "I was very curious about your reaction to my suggestion that God as pure act is synonymous with *Ipsum esse subsistens*. . . . Maybe the chill air of the North Country will stimulate your little grey cells and provide an answer." I confess I am still pondering that answer. Ralph went on to say, prophetically: "I hope I live long enough to see your book on God and, if not that, I will then be dealing with primary sources."

In 1964, I had accepted an offer to teach philosophy at Laval University (where I still teach). He had started at Notre Dame in 1955 and would stay there till the end of his life. Even though he quite understood my decision to join the Laval staff, a hint of tactful reproach for leaving Notre Dame was never far.

I am struck by the fact that in his last years he was able to write and publish, besides novels, the books he had most longed to write. I am thinking here of *Characters in Search of Their Author* and *Praeambula Fidei*, centering on God, and of *Dante and the Blessed Virgin*. To which I should add the monumental task of translating my father's works from the French under the title *The Writings of Charles De Koninck* at the Notre Dame Press. He was able to see the first two volumes come out in 2008 and 2009, respectively. And the last e-mail he sent me on 24 November 2009 reads as follows, "Dear Tom, I don't know if you have been kept informed of my recent descent into the valley. . . . An oesophageal cancer that they are confident they removed all traces of. . . . I shall leave the Mayo Clinic today, stay a few weeks with a daughter in Minneapolis, then home where I will put the final touches to vol. 3. . . . Maybe it was for that, that I was spared, Ralph."

Volume 2 begins with a translation of *"Ego Sapientia: The Wisdom that is Mary,"* and Volume 3 should contain two other "Marian books" by Charles De Koninck. On 21 May 2003, Ralph had written: "Do you realize I first went there [to Quebec] for summer school in 1950 [. . .] and your father's Marian writings were a first and permanent basis for my admiration and devotion to him." How fitting that Ralph's last book should have been devoted in part to the Blessed Virgin! Among the countless gems of *Dante and the Blessed Virgin*, and especially worth mentioning here, are Ralph's reflections on what St. Thomas calls "the

greatest spiritual good, the *gaudium caritatis,* or joy of charity."
Now the opposite of that greatest good is the capital sin of
sloth. To quote Ralph in *Dante and the Blessed Virgin,* "What is
necessary to understanding sloth is the recognition that there
is an order of spiritual goods, with the divine good being chief
among them. The special virtue of charity bears on the divine
good, and charity brings with it a joy in the divine good. Thus,
although any sin entails sadness with respect to a spiritual good,
sadness as to the acts consequent upon charity gives rise to the
special vice of *acedia"* (*ST* IIaIIae, q. 35, a. 2).

Those reflections were prompted by the passage in *Purgatorio*
18. 97–100 where one reads *Maria corse con fretta a la montagna:
Mary ran with haste to the mountain.* Part of the account Luke
gives of Gabriel's annunciation tells us that Mary set off
straightaway to visit her cousin Elizabeth. "The promptness of
Mary's act," Ralph comments, "makes it a model of zeal, the
virtue opposed to the vice of sloth." The zeal Ralph observed
in Mary was something he knew intimately—the key, I believe,
to the marvellous energy deployed in so many books, lectures,
and similar endeavours whose aim was to serve the common
good, the cause of education and culture, and above all the faith.

Meeting Ralph was almost invariably an occasion for
celebration. So were his letters and e-mails, bringing to mind
R. L. Stevenson's justly famous remark, in *The Lantern Bearers:*
"The true realism, always and everywhere, is that of the poets:
to find out where joy resides, and give it a voice far beyond
singing. For to miss the joy is to miss all." In his case it was
gaudium caritatis, "the joy of charity," that made all the difference.

*Thomas De Koninck is Professor of Philosophy in the Faculté de
philosophie of the Université Laval.*

A Medievalist with Passion, Commitment and a Wry Sense of Humor

In remembering Ralph McInerny, several themes immediately come to mind; first and foremost, the human qualities percolate to the top: his passion and commitment for philosophy, especially the philosophical work of Thomas Aquinas, all the while incorporating his marvelously wry sense of humor. Ralph took the realist insights of the work of Thomas Aquinas seriously; later philosophers would call this externalism developed through what John Haldane once referred to as the ontological and epistemological realism central to the meta-philosophy illustrated in the writings of Aquinas. At mid-century, it was Ralph who almost single handedly began his committed efforts to work with other philosophical traditions so that he could understand from whence they were coming and how to offer judicious Thomistic responses. It was Ralph with whom I had my first really serious discussion about how Aquinas provided an alternative to the standard naturalistic fallacy argument then so prominent in analytic philosophy. Ralph gave a principled response grounded in an analysis of a dispositional property from which the "good" was the *telos* of the dispositional property and not a property added on to a natural property like paint to a bench. I have never forgotten that discussion which took place in the living room of Aquinas House—how appropriate a place for that discussion!—during his visit to Ohio Dominican University now some twenty-five years ago.

If I may write personally for a moment, Ralph graciously served as an outside reader evaluating for possible publication my own manuscript on Aquinas and natural law for Oxford University Press. I still recall vividly seeing Ralph at a meeting of the American Catholic Philosophical Association, I think in St Louis, and he greeted my wife, Marianne and me saying, with some passion, "I told that lady in Oxford that she should publish your manuscript!" What a joyful utterance for an aspiring author to hear from an acknowledged master in the area of natural law theory! Later, when the book appeared, Ralph provided a thoughtful analytic review for *The Medieval Review*, which caught perspicuously the insights with which I had wrestled for some fifteen years.

Beyond these more or less private, personal events, my own work on natural law theory started to reach a degree of fruition and sophistication while attending the 1985 National Endowment for the Humanities Summer Institute on natural law theory in Aquinas that Ralph sponsored and directed. What a delightful month! In addition to his own work on Aquinas and moral theory, Ralph had invited John Finnis, Alan Donagan, Alasdair McIntyre, William Wallace, and Joe Boyle, among others, to work with those of us attending this Institute. Ralph, as always, was moved to integrate Thomistic insights into the wider world of philosophy. Not only did we have many chances to interact with those visiting lecturers, but also the informal discussions with the other budding philosophers attending the Institute were fruitful in ways that only later work would reveal.

The many Summer Thomistic Seminars too, always a week of intensive discussions on themes in the *omnia opera* of Aquinas, were phenomenally interesting and intellectually exciting. I was fortunate to attend more than several of these fascinating intellectual feasts and to read papers or offer comments at many. Ralph would select a theme, and then philosophers from around the Western world would descend on South Bend for a week of stimulating discussions and philosophical arguments. Platonic symposia would not have been better, to be sure.

Ralph certainly did have a bit of printer's ink in his veins. Reading his autobiography, *I Alone Have Escaped to Tell You*, one discovers that even at an early age, Ralph was seeking ways to express his literary and cultural insights and put these ideas onto paper. One is impressed at the more than several ways he undertook his significant research, especially during his early days as a philosopher at Notre Dame. Certainly his lovely wife and soul mate, Connie, assisted Ralph in enabling his philosophical and literary work to be undertaken with dispatch. His autobiography is an enriching narrative on these significant stays of study in Europe and the published results of those research ventures. Ralph's published philosophical work is duly impressive by any scholarly yardstick used to measure such work.

And the mystery tales! Ralph possessed a veritable knack for putting on the page gripping mystery narratives. In particular, I have enjoyed the Roger Knight series taking place on the campus of Notre Dame. The way Ralph would weave Notre Dame history and traditions into the narrative are always a delight to read. And Ralph could capture human idiosyncrasies of friends and colleagues with such perspicuity! His description of David Solomon's rushing through an office door to make a meeting brought tears of laughter to my eyes. I once told John Haldane that he had made a cameo appearance in one of Ralph's mysteries, which was news to Haldane. He was thrilled to know about this event, and he asked for the page reference so he could show his children. John was flattered, and he was not a person to flatter easily. Ralph's descriptive accounts of the "old goats" having lunch in the faculty club put on paper the dynamics of retired faculty discussions covering descriptively the many human and professional foibles unique to the members of our profession. One of my favorite academic novels, *Rogerson at Bay* (1976), dealt with Professor Robertson and his exploits at the Fort Elbow Branch of The Ohio State University, located somewhere due east of Fort Wayne! The account of Robertson's research project on "The Phenomenology of Jai Lai" still brings laughter to my mind. Ralph's keen eye for such human foibles must have been like Aquinas's *intellectus agens*—always on the go!

That wry wit could come forward in philosophical settings too. Who can forget his subtitle: *A Handbook for Peeping Thomists*! One of my early meetings with Ralph was when we were on a program together for a medieval conference in Cleveland. He and I were seated in the back of the room as a paper was being presented with the rather outlandish title of "The Theory of Universals from Parmenides to Ockham." Intuitively too much ground to cover, to be sure. But this venture started and the paper began, which was supposed to be a twenty-minute presentation. But the speaker droned on and on from one bit of unanalyzed data to another; Ralph finally bent over his chair in mild dismay as he quietly said: "This can't go on much longer—she'll run out of centuries!" That wry wit capturing a human—and academic—foible right at the center!

Indeed Ralph will be missed in philosophical circles. His commitment and passion for the realist philosophy of Thomas Aquinas was unrelenting and explicit. His judicious insights in sorting out philosophical conundrums were more often than not right on target. His writing was always direct and to the point, and overflowing with philosophical insights.

To Ralph McInerny, *Requiescat in Pace.*

Anthony J. Lisska is the Maria Theresa Barney Professor of Philosophy at Denison University and the author of Aquinas's Theory of Natural Law *(Oxford University Press, 1996).*

The Pursuit of Excellence

Ralph McInerny's genius (not too strong a word) manifested itself in whatever direction one turned, so that my instinct, instead of offering my recollection of him, is to advise people to go directly to the source—his own rich and fascinating autobiography with the title every would-be memoirist wishes he had thought of—*I Alone Have Escaped to Tell You.* As with most things, Ralph did it better than anyone else.

I first met him at Catholic University of America during the papal visit to the United States in 1979. As the assembled scholars were removing their robes after the address, someone remarked (not unkindly) that the speech had been a disappointment. "Nothing the pope does disappoints me," were the first words I ever heard Ralph McInerny utter. Not being a philosopher, I was not well acquainted with Ralph's scholarly works, but I knew he was a major figure in Thomistic circles, the head of the Maritain Center. He was also a kind of "public intellectual" who brought his scholarship to bear on all kinds of important contemporary questions.

Like most people who did not know him intimately, I was amazed to learn (eventually) of the sheer variety and volume of his activity—his almost literally countless number of books and articles, his membership on various Vatican commissions, the catholic distance university, International Catholic University he started and kept going, and his various summer institutes, to say nothing of the fact, mentioned casually, that he was a golfer. (What other hobbies did he never bother to mention?) Whenever we were together, for any reason, he always gave the impression that he had all the time in the world. When I asked the inevitable question of how he could do so much, he replied simply that he always carried a laptop computer and took advantage of a free half-hour here and there, often in airports. (But even he would not have been able to do all that he did without the highly efficient support of his long-time assistant Alice Osberger.)

Most scholars think of themselves as making their chief contribution to the world through their writings, and I am sure Ralph thought so as well. But instead of lamenting, like so many of us, the sad decline of Catholic intellectual life, Ralph saw a need and simply moved to fill it. His establishment of The Catholic distance university, his summer institutes on Basics of Catholicism, and his founding and editing of the journal *Catholic Dossier*, all things that carried demands for practical oversight, went beyond the call of duty. At a time when we lamented the absence of a serious Catholic journal in the United States, he and Michael Novak simply started *Catholicism in Crisis*. Ralph served several terms as president of the Fellowship of Catholic Scholars, then once again exceeded the call of duty by taking over the editorship of the organization's quarterly journal.

For some Catholics of my generation, the regnant Thomism of the 1950s often seemed abstract and remote from life, a perception that had much to do with the Catholic intellectual crisis that began around 1960. But when I got to know Ralph, many years later, I found him to be the embodiment of true humanism. I was vaguely familiar with Maritain's philosophy of art, but I was surprised at how deeply appreciative of literature Ralph was, indeed how passionate, although I confess that I still do not quite understand the connection between Thomism and the novels of Ralph's fellow St. Paul native F. Scott Fitzgerald. While everyone knew of Ralph's detective novels, I was amazed to learn from his memoir that he had been publishing fiction since the 1950s and had appeared in such places as *Redbook*, a magazine now forgotten but in its time a major outlet for commercial fiction. Some people might dismiss this achievement as a waste of time, or at best as a kind of intriguing trick, like Dr. Johnson's dog that could stand on its hind legs. But I think it revealed Ralph's deep humanism. It is one thing for a writer with a shallow commercial sensibility to produce such things, but for a genuine philosopher to do so indicates a broad human understanding, a remarkable ability to get outside oneself.

Ralph had an extremely dry and exquisite sense of humor. He dedicated one of his detective novels to my wife and me, and in another book a character claimed that Cardinal Wojtyla, before he was elected pope, had traveled semi-incognito in the United States, "staying with people like the Hitchcocks." (When asked if this was true, I always replied, "I'm not allowed to talk about it.") I made a cameo appearance in another of his novels, setting Garry Wills straight (herculean task indeed!) while chatting at a wake. I told Ralph I charged a standard fee for appearing in a novel.

While he had uncompromisingly critical judgment, I never heard him say anything uncharitable about an individual, nor did he ever resort to invective. In suavity of manner (and even to some extent physically) he rather reminded me of the English actor Wilfred Hyde-White. If it is a cliché to say, when someone dies, that it marks the passing of an era, in Ralph's case it is poignantly true. Nine years younger than Ralph, I began teaching at the very end of the Second Vatican Council, when the crisis of Catholic higher education (indeed of all higher education) had already begun.

Ralph, however, had started at Notre Dame a decade earlier, and he personally experienced the whole transition (if that is an adequate word). Although he accepted life with a serene joyfulness, that experience was a bitter and melancholy one for a man who had a deep devotion to Catholic higher education in general and to Notre Dame in particular. He told me that he had once been put in charge of the search for a new chairman of the Notre Dame theology department and, seeing a golden opportunity, worked hard to find suitable candidates, only to have a senior administrator tell him, almost casually, "Oh, don't worry about that, Ralph. We've found the man we want," a man who was not, needless to say, the man Ralph wanted.

As far as I could tell, Ralph's love of Notre Dame was almost total, and there is indeed a certain sad appropriateness that he should pass from the scene just after what would have been his last commencement ceremony, one that, for reasons all the world knows, he refused to attend.

It is merely the latest in a long series of ironies in Catholic higher education that, whereas institutions like Notre Dame transformed themselves under the mantra of the "pursuit of excellence," when Ralph's end came, the university could not acknowledge that, all along, he had been precisely one of its most distinguished exhibits of that elusive quality.

James Hitchcock is Professor of History at St. Louis University.

The Undergraduate Teacher

Ralph McInerny died on January 29, the day after the feast of St. Thomas Aquinas, to whom he had dedicated his life as a Catholic scholar and educator. Philosopher, teacher, novelist, poet, publisher, man of letters, activist, and father of six wonderful adult children (Ralph and Connie lost their first child, Michael, when he was just three years old), Ralph authored more than 100 books, along with countless scholarly articles and opinion columns. He is perhaps best known to the wider public for the 29 Father Dowling mysteries. But of special interest to lovers of Notre Dame is the series of 13 (if I haven't lost count!) mystery novels set on the Notre Dame campus and built around, so to speak, a rotund—to the point of being nearly immobile—professor of medieval studies and amateur sleuth named Roger Knight. And infusing all of this amazingly fruitful output was Ralph's deep Catholic faith and piety.

I'm not yet quite ready to write about what Ralph McInerny meant to me personally, and there is no need here to dwell on Ralph's distress over the way things have been going at Our Lady's university. Also best left for another occasion is Ralph's role as the benefactor of scores of graduate students and itinerant scholars, including a young and, at the time, penniless political refugee from a South American dictatorship now lionized by political progressives.

What I would like to focus on instead is Ralph's relationship with undergraduates at the university, especially over the last fifteen years or so. Since I myself served as director of undergraduate studies in philosophy for eight of those years, I can claim some first-hand knowledge whereof to speak.

For many years Ralph taught a 2-level philosophy course, open to majors and non-majors alike, called The Thought of Aquinas. Ralph was convinced, and ending up convincing others of us as well, that St. Thomas's system of wisdom, taken as a whole, is still the best foundation for the articulation of the Catholic claim to wisdom. The core of The Thought of Aquinas is contained in *A First Glance at St. Thomas Aquinas: A Handbook for Peeping Thomists* (1990), the book I usually recommend when undergraduates ask me which of Ralph's books about St. Thomas they should start with. (For more serious students who see themselves as budding Catholic intellectuals, I always recommend *Thomism in an Age of Renewal* (1968), which has nicely withstood the test of time. It's out of print, but you can still find used copies for sale online.)

Over the years Ralph also taught many seminars on St. Thomas for philosophy majors. For instance, his popular course on St. Thomas's moral theory is nicely encapsulated in *Ethica Thomistica* (1997), the best one-stop treatment of its subject matter. And in later years he specialized in dual (dueling?) figure courses with titles such as Dante and Aquinas, Newman and Aquinas, and Newman and Kierkegaard.

More interestingly perhaps, in the late 1990's Ralph's teaching took what might we might call a 'subversive' turn. In the spring of 1998, a group of eight students (and I know your names), looking for intellectual formation faithful to the teachings of the Church and not impressed with the regular course offerings in the philosophy and theology departments, asked Ralph to do a readings course with them on John Paul II's encyclicals *Veritatis Splendor* and *Evangelium Vitae*, along with the parts of St. Thomas relevant to the encyclicals. In subsequent semesters the number of students grew to thirty and the topics included the documents of Vatican II, the philosophical underpinnings of the social encyclicals of the twentieth century, the encyclical *Fides et Ratio*, and so on. They would meet in the Maritain Center under the cover of night—Nicodemus-style, so to speak—and there were always refreshments. This 'shadow curriculum' continued into the new century and, ironically, evoked in some of us oldsters memories of student discontent with the 'official curriculum' in the 1960's. In any case, a good time was had by all, and those courses helped nurture a number of priestly and religious vocations, along with a lot of solid Catholic marriages.

Now for the dark side. As one might expect, Ralph's unrelenting promotion of authentic Catholic teaching earned him more than a few campus enemies. When in 1982 he and Michael Novak launched the magazine *Catholicism in Crisis* in the wake of what they took to be an imprudent and skewed pastoral letter by the American bishops on nuclear deterrence, then University President Fr. Hesburgh received a hefty stack of protest letters from disgruntled faculty members. In 1997, when Ralph sponsored a series of lectures meant to explain and defend the Church's teaching on homosexuality and the treatment of homosexuals, the head of Campus Ministry took to the pages of *The Observer* to advise undergraduates not to attend. ("He didn't bother to call me," I remember Ralph complaining. "I've never even met the guy.") There was lots of other whining about Ralph over the years as well. The criticism might have bothered him to some degree, but it never deterred him. Like Peter and John before him, he rejoiced at being "judged worthy of ill-treatment for the sake of the Name" (Acts 5:41). And through it all, he never lost his wit or his wits. Besides, he had his own built-in way of exacting humorous vengeance: in his novels.

Much of the good work that Ralph initiated with undergraduates has been continued and expanded upon by his dear friend David Solomon of the Notre Dame Center for Ethics and Culture. And this continuity was a source of great consolation for Ralph as he retired last year after 53 years of teaching at Notre Dame. Every year, the Center for Ethics and Culture sponsors a fall lecture series on important Catholic (and, this past fall, "almost Catholic") literary figures. My suspicion is that there will sometime soon be a lecture on the literary legacy of Ralph McInerny.

The congregation at Ralph's funeral included many friends and former students who had traveled long distances from all over the country. The aforementioned political refugee, now teaching in Chile, wanted very badly to come, but found that only business class airline tickets were available on such short notice for the flight from Santiago to New York. You just know that if Ralph McInerny had been alive, he would have sent the money for that ticket to his own funeral.

Alfred J. Freddoso is the John and Jean Oesterle Professor of Thomistic Studies at the University of Notre Dame. This essay first appeared in the February 8, 2010, issue of The Irish Rover, *a student-run newspaper at Notre Dame.*

Letter of Gratitude

Professor Ralph McInerny was mentor to an era. Every Catholic who valued the conversation between faith and reason related to Ralph, either personally or through his voluminous writings, or both.

More, Prof. McInerny's lived witness to faith's reaching to the limits of human experience and then beyond encouraged us all and will be grievously missed; but if Ralph's many fictional characters are also ideas in God's mind, heaven is a lively place where Ralph will be perfectly at home.

I offer my condolences to his family and join in their prayers for his eternal rest and joy in the Lord.

This letter from Francis Cardinal George, Archbishop of Chicago, was read aloud at Ralph's funeral reception.

A Mosaic Bing Crosby

Many will write of Ralph's impressive scholarship and diverse interests. I will write some about Ralph's accomplishments but I want to write mostly about Ralph as a person, a friend and mentor. I am, however, one of the few who thinks she knows how Ralph managed to have such prodigious scholarly and popular output. I am convinced his mind was working full steam on several tracks at the same time; it was churning out puns and witticisms constantly; it was working on the latest novel; it was solving complex philosophical problems, processing profound and sometimes poetic thoughts, and it was fully focused on whomever he was talking with—all at the same time. Now how you do that?! I don't know, but I think that was what he was capable of doing. To the question, "Is the light on when the refrigerator door is closed," the answer—if Ralph is the refrigerator—is "Yes—and there are several ice makers doing their job at all times, as well."

It was not hard to love Ralph. He was simultaneously suave, sophisticated, urbane, relaxed, welcoming, and down-to-earth. He was tremendously and effortlessly charming. Recently, I saw just a few minutes of an old Bing Crosby movie and the resemblances seemed to me to be startling. His romantic interest said to the ever debonair Bing, "You are so charming, sincere, and stable." That is a good list to commence complimenting Ralph. Bing was also always ready to burst into some comforting, mellifluous song that seemed to put the world right, and so it was with Ralph; he seemed to have the perfect words for all occasions. Bing and Ralph both had a look of benign mischief in their eyes; you knew that at any minute you could be in for some gentle teasing that would serve somehow to build you up, not tear you down.

Bing captures the grounded but light hearted side of Ralph—the side that was expressed by his joyful sauntering through life. For the intense purpose-driven life that Ralph led, Moses comes to mind as the fitting analogue. Both undertook the mission of leading many to the promised land. Ralph was acutely aware, more than anyone I have known, that he was building on the work of his forefathers, for whose work he expressed pious gratitude, and knew he had an obligation to shape those who were to carry on the work in future generations. In a sense, his life was an unrelenting effort to remind us of eternal truths and our obligation to do what we could to preserve them, understand them deeply, build on them, and pass them onto others. For many summers he ran both a summer workshop for accomplished and for up-and coming Thomists and a workshop on Basic Catholicism for those who couldn't find reliable presentations of fundamental Catholicism anywhere. (Isn't it wonderful that those days are over? In part thanks to Ralph's solace and training of many.) Summer after summer he sat in the front row in rapt attention for talks he had heard countless times or talks he could have given much much better. Always full of compliments to the speakers; always spectacularly accessible to the attendees. And we would find that at the end of the week, he had somehow found time to write another book. That multi-tracked mind!

It would be easy to exhaust one's supply of positive adjectives in describing Ralph. I am confident that all who write tributes to him will mention his kindness since that was perhaps his most salient characteristic—after his manifest intelligence. Much of his kindness was *sub tabula*. I remember watching Ralph ask a poor young scholar at a conference if she would be at the banquet; she made some lame excuse (which I did not recognize as lame) for an inability to attend. Not long after we parted, I saw a conference organizer approach her with an "extra" ticket for the event. I knew Ralph had purchased one for her. For years he attended to the widowed Jean Oesterle like she was his mother; he helped find scholarly projects that kept her going, gave her an office nearby, and doted on her with his daily friendship. I am sure these examples could be multiplied exponentially.

Ralph was marvelous to me during my trials at Notre Dame. He befriended me when I was a raw recruit in the fight for the good and true and never acted like he was the "great man" supporting the clueless newbie. He always treated me as an equal, although I knew I was privileged to have him as a mentor and friend. His "mentoring" was of the most subtle kind; in fact, I learned most simply by being in his company and observing him deal with people. It was also most edifying to watch him hatch new improbable schemes and seemingly make them materialize overnight. I remember his wife, Connie, and me agreeing that very few people wake up each morning with a new grand idea for saving Western Civilization or for putting an end to dissent in the Church and there are fewer who make most of them happen, but Ralph was that kind of guy.

When I was denied tenure at Notre Dame, Ralph was prepared to spearhead an effort to challenge the decision and even went to consult a lawyer with me. I admit I didn't know whether his foremost motive was to support me or to gather material for some impending novel. And he wasn't nice only to those who occupied the same ecclesial camp as himself; he was notorious for championing anyone who he thought got a raw deal, among them a prominent feminist whom he used to debate about the possibility of women becoming priests. When she was denied tenure, he battled for her.

Ralph never backed away from a fight, yet never was pugnacious or belligerent. He was always the gentleman, always fair, always gracious. Indeed, he was undeniably more fair to his opponents than they were to him, both his opponents in the scholarly world and those in the Church. I doubt that anyone could accuse Ralph of underhanded behavior. Still, he didn't hesitate to use his resources to advance the causes and people he believed in but, again, transparently and fairly. When Notre Dame started becoming friendly to the political maneuvering of the gay/lesbian lobby, he arranged for a series of speakers on campus who defended Church teaching. It infuriated many, but Ralph doggedly reverenced the Church and its authority more than he reverenced the trendy irreverent climbers at Notre Dame.

I remember a wonderful quodlibetal ("ask whatever you like") session at the University of Dallas where Ralph fielded questions with the finesse of Roger Federer returning brilliant volleys. That's when I realized that those who are in the top 1% of intelligent people can easily make those who are in the top 2% look like fools if they want to. Ralph didn't want to but you knew there was phenomenal power behind that charm. Ralph didn't want to flatten anyone. He just wanted to lay out the truth so carefully and clearly that rejecting it would seem simply foolish. Ralph made the world seem a more intelligible and friendlier place by conveying the attitude that a lot of it does make sense if you just use your mind to think about it—and embrace and trust the Catholic faith! His clarity and certainty about truth did not tend toward dogmatic closure on questions. The truth we know is just a stepping stone to further knowledge, knowledge cloaked in beauty and wonder, and those privileged to have minds trained to discover it were obliged to do so and pass that knowledge on to others, with an equal combination of humility and determination. Ralph's humility and determination inspired others to imitate his approach to the search for understanding.

Connie, refreshingly candid and delightfully feisty in her own right, was the perfect wife for Ralph. At home, they entertained beautifully together. It was a pleasure to be invited to events on Portage Avenue attended by many of the old guard at Notre Dame. The intimate and warm friendships were a comfort to all; the conversations were erudite, hilarious and captivating.

I hope it is not irreverent, but in fact Ralph reminded me a lot of God (after all, we are supposed to be as perfect as our heavenly Father is perfect). God is harder at work than any of us; involved in projects galore, but always ready to interrupt those projects to help us achieve our ends. And God seems to be equal work and play; he not only instructs and helps us constantly, he continually provides us with things to delight us. So, of course, did Ralph. I never knew who the "real" Ralph was, whether he was a philosopher or a mystery writer at heart. But, like God, he seemed to want to give us some very serious food for the mind and then to give us some enchanting frivolity as a complementary palate cleanser.

I count Ralph among those who stood by me and shaped me. I know there are countless others who have been the beneficiaries of his goodness. I know his children must feel infinitely blessed to have had him and Connie as their parents; his colleagues and friends at Notre Dame must feel infinitely blessed to have had him as colleague and friend. We were all immeasurably blessed to have had Ralph in our lives; we pray now that he is enjoying truly infinite blessings in the arms of the Truth he loved and defended so well.

Janet Smith holds the Fr. Michael J. McGivney Chair of Life Issues at the Sacred Heart Major Seminary in Detroit and is the author of Life Issues, Medical Choices, *among other books.*

Everything Is Different

Our dear friend died at age eighty of complications, weeks after surgery for esophageal cancer. To say that he will be sorely missed and that he leaves a gaping hole in Catholic intellectual life are the kinds of things that might be said about several people. But Ralph was like no one else. In fact, given his great achievements in philosophy, fiction writing, poetry, journalism, teaching, translation, and other fields (not least humor), his passing is like the disappearance of several highly talented people. You can imagine him writing a clever detective story in which friends who knew a person in one capacity are shocked to find out after he dies that they knew only a small slice of a multifaceted character. There may indeed be people who have precisely that experience at his funeral mass in the Basilica of the Sacred Heart on the campus of the University of Notre Dame, where he was a phenomenon for over half a century.

In this book, there are remembrances of those who knew him at Notre Dame as well as elsewhere. If Ralph were still alive, he might find this a bit embarrassing because he was the least self-centered of men. To be sure, he knew what he had done and he liked to talk about it, especially the books that had fallen into relative obscurity. But you often had the sense that he, too, was surprised that he'd been lucky enough to create such wonderful things, was happy he had, yet felt as a matter of course that such things are not, in the end, reason to boast, but gifts from God.

We were together once at EWTN to tape some shows. After breakfast, we went to our rooms to work until we had to appear. Ralph emerged about two hours later, a kind of standard writing session for him, with a dazed smile on his face, "I didn't expect it to go that well." All writers have days when they suffer the torments of hell just to produce a few ordinary paragraphs. Ralph seemed to have fewer such days than anyone else.

His autobiography *I Alone Have Escaped to Tell You: My Life and Pastimes* manages to give you in a very few lively pages the history of Ralph and his family – his time in a seminary, his decision to study philosophy, travels around the world, his often nocturnal work habits – as if even he thought of all of it as just interesting material for which he was not bragging or trying to make himself any more than he already was in readers' minds. But almost anyone who picks it up will be "unable to put it down." I gave it to my wife and some of my children, who have quite different tastes and interests, as a kind of experiment to see how Ralph's magic would work outside the usual readership. It worked like a charm.

It was typical of his generous spirit that he told me (after helping, with Michael Novak, to get *The Catholic Thing* off the ground by sending us a small sum still sitting in the account of the Orestes Brownson Institute at Notre Dame) that he didn't need or want any payment for columns. We pay so little that it's maybe not as great a sacrifice as it might seem. But a regular contributor who is not getting paid might be tempted to skip a deadline here and there. Ralph, never. Once he made a commitment, he delivered. Before he went to the Mayo Clinic for his operation, he sent several columns (you may not have noticed at the time, but re-read "We Lepers" (http://www.thecatholicthing.org/content/view/1902/2/) in light of Ralph's own intimations of mortality, with its conclusion "Notionally, mortality is a pretty dull fact. But it is a feature of life that certain limit situations bring home to us its reality. It is no longer notional. What then? Like Damien, we go on doing what we were doing. Yet everything is different.").

He had calculated out how long his convalescence would take and sent enough columns to appear normally in the regular rotation until he could start writing again. When convalescence took longer than he'd hoped, he let me know that he still expected to be back in 2010. I said I'd hold him to that. Sadly, it didn't work out. But his spirit will always be a part of the writers and readers of *The Catholic Thing*, as he's part of the lives of hundreds of thousands of people around the world – now, perhaps, even more than in life.

Rest in peace, dear Ralph, and flights of angels–O lucky angels!–take thee to thy rest.

Robert Royal is editor-in-chief of The Catholic Thing, *and president of the Faith & Reason Institute in Washington, D.C. His most recent book is* The God That Did Not Fail: How Religion Built and Sustains the West. *This contribution originally appeared on* thecatholicthing.org.

A Man of Virtue

One of the marks of a virtuous character, according to Aristotle, is the performance of virtuous acts with ease and delight. On that basis, as well as others, Ralph McInerny was a remarkably virtuous man. One of Ralph's most beautiful books is entitled *The Very Rich Hours of Jacques Maritain: A Spiritual Life*, the premise of which is that "we can find in the person of Jacques Maritain a model of the intellectual life in the pursuit of sanctity." Those words certainly apply to Ralph, one of the great Catholic intellectuals of our time. What distinguished Ralph was not just his fidelity, his intelligence, and his astonishing productivity, but his gracious and ready wit. He possessed a knack for conversation with everyone—from philosophers and politicians, to the elderly and children. Unlike most gifted individuals, Ralph was never burdened by his gifts. He engaged in serious pursuits joyfully, almost playfully.

Ralph excelled in so many spheres and combined so many virtues in his person that it is difficult to know where to begin in recounting his noteworthy achievements. He was a philosopher (author of more than two dozen scholarly books, he gave the prestigious Gifford Lectures in 1999–2000), a translator (he translated the texts of Aquinas for Penguin Classics), a critically acclaimed and popular novelist (author of a number of mystery series, including the popular Father Dowling series that became a television series), a public intellectual (he appeared on William F. Buckley's *Firing Line*, and was a member of President George W. Bush's Committee on the Arts and Humanities), a journalist (with Michael Novak, he founded *Crisis*, a journal of lay Catholic opinion), and a published poet. In the midst of all this activity, Ralph was remarkably generous with his time and his help, especially for his students, in whose families he expressed an avid interest.

In recent years after the death of his beloved wife Connie, with whom he had seven children, his thoughts turned increasingly to age and death. In a wonderful and deeply autobiographical volume of poems, *The Soul of Wit*, he reflected at length on death. He said often that since Connie died, he felt posthumous. They were indeed a perfect match. As a graduate student, I met Connie when Ralph introduced her by saying, "Have you met my first wife?" With a wit as quick as Ralph's, she had no trouble keeping up. Even or especially when occupied with thoughts of easeful death, Ralph's humor emerged. He liked to tell the story about a hospital visit to see a failing Jean Oesterle, his Notre Dame colleague, a convert to the faith, and a translator of Aquinas. Hesitantly, he asked, "Jean, do you know who I am?" She retorted, "Don't you know?"

Ralph had an indiscriminate love of puns; he seemed to enjoy bad puns more than good ones—a thesis that would seem to be confirmed by a perusal of the titles of his mystery novels (*On This Rockne, Irish Gilt, Law and Ardor, Rest in Pieces*, or *The Book of Kills*). An appreciation for the nuances and richness of ordinary language informed not only his humor but also his practice of philosophy. His most important philosophical text was *Aquinas and Analogy*, a study of the way Thomas Aquinas, following Aristotle, teased out of the complexity of ordinary language unities of meaning. He rejected the idea that Thomas Aquinas provided us with a philosophical system intended to compete with other systems. Instead, Thomas was asking in a more precise way questions every human being asks; he is interested in the human good, not the good of professional philosophers or intellectuals. In keeping with this working assumption, Ralph wrote both for elite groups of scholars and for intrigued laymen. With the latter group in mind, he penned *A First Glance at Thomas Aquinas: A Handbook for Peeping Thomists.* His distinctive approach to Thomas Aquinas is most evident in his supple account of natural law (see *Ethica Thomistica,* for example), and in his defense of natural theology in the text of his Gifford Lectures, published as *Characters in Search of Their Author,* the thesis of which Ralph states thus: "For us it is all but inevitable that, however momentarily, we feel ourselves to be part of a vast cosmic drama and our thoughts turn to the author, not merely of our roles, but of our existence. Natural theology is one version of that quest." Ralph's philosophical work flourished at the University of Notre Dame, to which he moved in 1955, after receiving his doctorate at Laval under the great Thomist Charles DeKoninck and teaching for one year at Creighton. His first office at Notre Dame was in the administration building, the Golden Dome. When he and a colleague became intrigued by the presence of an old safe, they opened it, and, amid the clutter, discovered a draft of a novel written by Knute Rockne, a novel dedicated to Arnold McInerny. At Notre Dame, he held an endowed chair as the Michael P. Grace Professor of Medieval Studies; he was also director of the Maritain Center and of the Medieval Institute.

Early on at Notre Dame, he began, in addition to his teaching and philosophical work, to write fiction. The story of how he made the transition from wanting to be a writer to becoming one is illuminating. After a time in which he haphazardly polished off and sent out short stories for publication, only to receive rejection letters, he decided that he would write daily over the next year. If nothing were accepted for publication, he would take that as a sign it was not meant to be. So, every evening, after he had put his children to bed, he would repair to his unfinished basement and stand, not sit, before his typewriter pecking away from 10 p.m. to 2 a.m. On the wall in front of him, he had posted these words in bold, "No One Owes You a Reading." He eventually published some short stories and then had a breakthrough in 1969 with *The Priest,* a work that became a *New York Times* bestseller. He wrote more than eighty novels and received the Bouchercon Lifetime Achievement Award for mystery writing.

Ralph's life and career will always be enmeshed with the university he loved, Our Lady's University. He was of course deeply chagrined at the direction of the University. The concerns about Notre Dame's Catholic identity have become very public in the past few years with the administration's decisions to elevate the tawdry *Vagina Monologues* to the status of great art and to award an honorary doctorate of laws to a pro-abortion president. Before all that, Ralph objected to the premature firing of Coach Tyrone Willingham, in an *New York Times* op-ed piece "The Firing Irish," and to the unseemly image of a president and priest chasing down potential coaches on airport tarmacs in the dead of night. Even prior to that, Ralph objected to hiring practices that focused exclusively on "academic" criteria and rendered irrelevant knowledge of, and sympathy for, the Catholic faith and intellectual tradition. For Ralph, the accelerating abandonment of things Catholic at Notre Dame was the direct result of a craven quest for success understood in conventional, and often quite secular, terms.

It is common to say that Notre Dame's motto is "God, Country, Notre Dame," but Ralph was quick to remind us that the official motto is *"vita, dulcedo et spes"*—words meaning "life, sweetness, and hope" from the Latin Marian prayer, *Salve Regina*. How fitting that Ralph's last book, published just months ago, is *Dante and the Blessed Virgin*. Again, what he said of Jacques Maritain is equally true of Ralph. Teacher of teachers, he was a "model of the Christian philosopher, of the Thomist, both by what he taught and what he was."

Thomas S. Hibbs is Distinguished Professor of Ethics and dean of the honors college at Baylor University. He finished his dissertation under the direction of Ralph McInerny in 1987.

An Old Sinner

In the fall of 2006, Our Lady of the Road was in deep trouble. We at the Catholic Worker in South Bend had been kicked out of our neighborhood the year before, we had purchased two houses in another neighborhood to provide hospitality to the handful of guests we take in each night, and, in an attempt to continue helping others on the street (coffee, breakfast, showers, and a place to do laundry), we had purchased an old auto parts store and warehouse on Main Street for a day-time, drop-in center. We had hired a construction company to do the renovations, but the price tag was running higher than predicted. We were coming to know existentially the meaning of the familiar phrase "cost overrun." Facing a two-month deadline for our opening, and the construction company's demand for partial payment on the work competed, we had to come up with $15,000. Where would we get the money?

I was stewing on this question while reciting psalms for Sunday morning Lauds, running the various options through my head. Our usual donors? They were maxed out on our begging. First Source Bank? They wouldn't sign on to our Sermon-on-the-Mount approach to what they call "donor-based revenue streams." Notre Dame? An unlikely prospect; I'd already been informed that the University was knee-deep in under-funded community projects and wouldn't be taking on another. Jumping back and forth from thoughts of our cash crunch to psalm verses ("I was hard pressed and was falling, but the Lord came to help me"), I noticed the clock: 9:45. Time to go to Mass at Holy Cross, a quiet, no-frills, no-music assemblage of mainly grey-headed old-timers; over in less than an hour. I was in no mood for anything elaborate. The Mass went as usual. On the way out, while dipping into the holy water font, I ran into Ralph McInerny. "Want to come over for coffee?" he asked, "I live just down the street."

I first heard about Ralph long before ever meeting him. In the early eighties, when I was at Moreau Seminary, he created a stir on campus by starting a magazine called *Catholicism in Crisis*. At the time, I was taking a seminar on Reinhold Niebuhr taught by Stanley Hauerwas, so I caught the allusion to the journal's agenda: just as Niebuhr had challenged liberal Protestants with his version of neo-orthodoxy, so Ralph and Michael Novak were set on challenging liberal Catholicism with their particular Catholic version of neo-orthodoxy, including, as the early first issues made clear, taking a hard-line stance toward the Soviet Union. Years later, in grad school at Duke, I read an article on Ralph in *Notre Dame Magazine* in which he referred to himself as "a Thomist of the strict observance." "Too philosophical a reading of Thomas," I hastily surmised, having read my de Lubac; too Aristotelian, not Augustinian enough. By the time I returned to the Notre Dame campus in 1996, I'd come to appreciate the resistance to secularization he represented, but still, when I chatted with him, I'd leave mystified by his trust in reason, his romance with "nature." I was amused, however, by the way he addressed me: "Hello, Father," with an inflection that felt like an admonition. He was man of the Church.

As we strolled on this beautiful autumn day to his house in Holy Cross Village, he explained why he bought it. With his wife Connie gone, he wanted a smaller place, a short walk to Notre Dame's campus. His sitting room was lined with books, and there was a garage full nearby. Over coffee and half a pack of cigarettes, we talked about Maritain, Gilson, and the great controversy among Thomist circles in Europe during the thirties: Is there a Christian philosophy? Ralph argued Maritain's position with a subtlety and nuance that I hadn't encountered in grad school. Aristotle and Aquinas came up, as did de Koninck and Dante. At a lull in the conversation, with some apprehension, I took the opportunity to explain why I had petitioned for a return to the lay state. He responded graciously, generously, recalling how when in the seminary it became clear to him that celibacy was not his cup of tea. The only question he asked was whether or not I was still obligated to say the office. I told him I didn't think so.

As the conversation wound down—I sensed he wanted to get some reading or writing done—I brought up the matter I had been fretting about that morning. "Ralph, I was wondering if you might be willing to help the Catholic Worker, maybe get some of your friends to help too. You see, we have these bills hanging over our heads . . ." "How much do you need?" "$15,000." He walked over to his desk, sat down, wrote out a check, and handed it to me. I couldn't resist looking at it: the full amount. "Ralph, I didn't expect you to"—but he interrupted: "No problem. Glad to help." I walked back to my car at the church with a spring in my step.

Over the next few years, we turned to Ralph periodically for help with Our Lady of the Road. He came down one afternoon to see our houses, shaking his head. "I could never do this." Another time, he brought us arm loads of suits and shirts, after which we went to lunch. At my behest, he shared his views on natural law. The problem with natural law theorists, he explained, is that they try to erect a theory for what we already know. Referring to Notre Dame's embattled president on the touchy issue of *The Vagina Monologues*, he scoffed at the idea of forming a committee. "He should have asked his mother!" When I asked how he could endorse Reagan's Star Wars nuclear defense policy, he said it was the only way he could sleep at night. His version of natural law was marked with wit and a breezy confidence, some said too breezy. On the other hand, one of his contributions to the Catholic Worker was folded into a page of stationery containing a simple request, written in the handwriting of an aging man well aware of what lay ahead: "Pray for an old sinner." His confidence came from beyond himself.

The last time Ralph came down to the Worker was about a year before he died. We sat in my attic office for two hours discussing the influence on Dorothy Day of the dark spiritual roots of Huysmans, a late-nineteenth-century convert to Catholicism whose pre-conversion period involved dalliances with prostitutes and dabbling in black masses. All that seemed far removed from the blithe, confident embrace of the Faith that had carried Ralph through six decades of raising a family, producing dozens of tomes on Aristotle and Aquinas, and writing mystery novels on the side. The last few pot boilers, as it turned out, included characters involved in the Catholic Worker; one is a guy who is drawn away from the dingy, disheveled environs of a soup kitchen by the charms of a beautiful, well-to-do woman with whom he sips wine in Napa Valley (George Worth in *Relic of*

Time). And the last Notre Dame mystery, *Sham Rock* (not yet published at the time of Ralph's death) has a young Notre Dame grad turning her art studio in downtown Minneapolis into a soup kitchen called, alas, Our Lady of the Road. People had warned that if you hang around Ralph long enough, you'll eventually find yourself in one of his novels. A disturbing encounter it is, to see yourself as others see you—except in Ralph's novels, the characters are placed in comic plotlines, the conflicts get resolved. All's well that ends well.

I thought of those plotlines as Ralph passed through the doors of Sacred Heart one final time, accompanied by the ancient chant pointing to a life well lived, *In paradisum deducant te angeli*. A life not without its tragedies, of course: for Ralph, the loss of a son buried in Cedar Grove Cemetery five decades earlier; the loss of his wife, buried nearby five years earlier, the dissipated mission of the university he called home ("they think they own the place," he'd quip of the trustees). Still, his faith, amid such tragedies, was by all accounts undaunted, Catholic to the end. He had found what the ancients had long sought: a happy death. He knew—and imparted the knowledge to us as we walked away from Cedar Grove that cold winter morning—that the story does not end there.

Michael Baxter teaches theology at Notre Dame and is working on a book entitled The Sign of Peace: Essays on War, Peace, and Conscience in Catholic Tradition.

After McInerny

Among the philosophers of my own generation to whom I am indebted no one holds a higher place than Ralph McInerny. It was thanks to him that I finally became a Thomist. I had been introduced to Aquinas some 25 years before I first encountered either Ralph or his writings. But during that time I had become an Aristotelian and I had been too easily persuaded by a variety of Thomists, among them Gilson, that Aquinas was not an Aristotelian. I valued Aquinas's commentaries on Aristotle, especially that on the *Nicomachean Ethics*, but I had failed to recognize how Aquinas was making Aristotle's words his own.

It was Ralph who patiently and incisively and wittily disabused me of my errors—or at least of this particular part of them, so that I came to understand not only that Aquinas is the finest interpreter of Aristotle, but that Thomism is what Aristotelianism had to become, if it was to transcend its limitations, the limitations of Aristotle's time, place, and prejudices, and if it was to extend its questioning into further areas of enquiry.

Ralph in his own philosophical enquiries was at one with Aristotle and Aquinas in his insistence on beginning where we are, inviting us to join him and them in articulating more adequately than we had done so far thoughts that were already ours, even if not yet spelled out, knowledge that was already ours, but not yet acknowledged. So a key to his own thought—I am tempted to say the key, but that would be going too far—is the lecture that he gave in Palermo in 2004 on implicit moral knowledge (*Conoscenza Morale Implicita: Implicit Moral Knowledge*, Catanzaro: Rubbettino 2005), where the starting point for his argument is Aristotle's thesis that, in demonstrating any truth, we rely on "principles which are not known in this way," truths of which we have preexistent knowledge.

The first principles on which all our demonstration, all our argument relies, are presupposed by everything that we assert from our earliest utterances onwards and, given what our earliest utterances in fact were—Ralph here adverts to the evidence concerning his own first utterances as an infant and those of his children—we may be very surprised by this. So we need to reflect philosophically, if we are to recognize that in asserting anything at all we had already exhibited an implicit and inchoate knowledge of being and of the truth that "something cannot be and not be at the same time and in the same respect."

Where practical knowledge, moral knowledge, knowledge of what is to be done or not done, is concerned, our implicit knowledge of the first principle of practical reasoning, that good is to be done and evil avoided, is already presupposed in our earliest practical judgments. Our knowledge of which actions are good and which evil "is embedded in the practices of our upbringing. It is a knowledge, certainly, but it is often the all but unarticulated knowing that doing involves." So here once more there is work for philosophical reflection. And there are especially important consequences for how we think about the relationship of teachers to students.

A teacher is not imparting to students truths of which up to that point they have been wholly ignorant. She or he is eliciting from those students an awareness of knowledge that they already possess, but do not know that they possess. A good teacher, therefore, puts her or his students to the question in such a way that they become self-questioners, entering into a Socratic dialogue with themselves. And Ralph was often just such a teacher, a teacher of those who became self-teachers and later, sometimes, the teachers of others. So he developed in his students habits, qualities of mind and character, that enabled them to become themselves as teachers rather than copies of him.

The same attitudes and convictions informed his stance as a controversialist, a stance that combined, on the one hand, firmness and argumentative ruthlessness with respect to the moral truths that he was defending with, on the other, courtesy and considerateness towards those whom he took to be in moral error. For he recognized that their quarrel was primarily with themselves and not with him and that his task was to get them, too, to recognize this by eliciting from them an acknowledgment of what they knew perfectly well, but were strenuously denying that they knew.

It was important to Ralph that *everyone* begins from this unspelled out knowledge of moral truths and that everyone, therefore, has the resources to direct themselves, in the company of others, towards the achievement of that happiness which is their final good. This was not, on the view taken by the large majority of Aristotle scholars, Aristotle's view. Those scholars, therefore, presented a challenge which Ralph met with careful exegesis in his too little known "Some Reflections on Aristotle and Elitism" (*The Review of Metaphysics,* March 2008), where he argued that Aristotle recognizes other paths to contemplative activity than those taken by philosophers, paths which it is open to every human being to take. And he found in the *Poetics* a recognition by Aristotle that poetry, especially tragedy, "is a way to get an intimation of the divine . . . open to both philosophers and other citizens—and necessary to both."

No one could, in Ralph's view, do without poetry. For the poet, like the novelist, makes it possible for us to see and hear what habit and familiarity have rendered invisible and inaudible. Orhan Pamuk in his Nobel Lecture remarked that "A writer talks of things that everyone knows but does not know they know." Pamuk was not of course talking, as Plato, Aristotle, Aquinas, and McInerny do, of that knowledge which we already possess in our earliest judgments, but of that knowledge which we need if we are to see and hear things as they are. Writers achieve this in various ways, not least by the comic devices of parody and exaggeration, at which we are apt to laugh, at least until we realize that those parodies and exaggerations are *us*, that we have been laughing at ourselves. In his use of those devices in the best of his novels Ralph was as masterly in the exercise of his arts as he was in his philosophy.

Ralph the philosopher and Ralph the novelist sometimes appeared on the same stage, when what begins as a philosophical example threatens to take on a fictional life of its own. So it is with his adventures on the Indiana Toll Road with Fifi La Rue—perhaps, he carefully notes, her stage name—or with the sequence of events that begins with a robin kicking from its nest an unhatched egg and ends with Ralph lying "bloody and inert upon the greensward" or with Seymour who is growing a beard, all of them unlikely, but illuminating intrusions upon the expositions and arguments of *Ethica Thomistica*.

Add to Ralph the philosopher and Ralph the novelist and poet Ralph the friend, as excellent at friendship as at philosophy and at writing novels and poems. As time goes on, I shall miss him more and more.

Alasdair MacIntyre, the author of many books including After Virtue, *is the Rev. John A. O'Brien Senior Research Professor of Philosophy at the Notre Dame Center for Ethics and Culture at the University of Notre Dame.*

Professor, Artist, Editor, Publisher, Translator, Holy Man, Gentleman, Friend to a Multitude, and a Helluva Companion for Laughter and Story

Our friend Ralph has slipped behind the clouds, out where the Sun is brightest. He will still be with us.

I can't think of any man in our time who accomplished more in one lifetime, in more different spheres, with a wider array of talents. He seemed to be laughing all the time. No one was so steady a gusher of puns, not least in the titles of his novels: *On This Rockne, Frigor Mortis, The Emerald Aisle* . . . even in his introduction to the philosophy of St. Thomas Aquinas, his guide for "Peeping Thomists."

A dinner with Ralph was a feast of stories. Also, probes by him to follow up on his curiosities. Also, seeking your opinions. Tales of the latest "progressive" outrages, followed by kind words for the particular persons being singled out. New projects he was thinking of, and what do you think of this? Puns, of course, and an endless appetite for new funny stories and the telling of the latest of his own.

One always left Ralph warmed by his love for the Church. That love may have been his most distinguishing characteristic. It surely fed his zest for the comedic sense of the Divine. It won his gratitude for the great intellectual patrimony it brought him.

He had great patience for me when I was swinging left, both politically and theologically. Nor did he gloat when experience brought me back toward love for orthodoxy (not passive, but inquisitive and pioneering) and political realism. He wryly smiled at the proposed title for my intellectual journey: *Writing from Left to Right.*

Ralph's course was always steadier. He let people pass him by on left and right, and observed the wreckage as he later passed them by. He changed a lot himself, of course. But often he was just remaining constant as the world veered left and right, to extremes. He watched his hereditary Democratic Party adopt old Republican tendencies such as isolationism, while Republicans (*mirabile dictu*) became pro-life and rather more Catholic all the time. Ralph did not think social justice, the common good, and subsidiarity pointed to ever larger government. He had a mid-western habit of common sense and a steady observation of results, rather than self-admiring motives.

There is a largeness about the American Middle West, and the sky there is very tall above the silos, water tanks, and trees. What counts there is feet on the ground, and not getting too big for thine own britches. There is a contemplative spirit there, and the steadiness of the rich soil all around. There is a distinctive Catholic spirituality of the middle part of the United States. Ralph lived it.

He suffered a lot from his wife Connie's death. She was always so matter-of-fact, down-to-earth, and a wifely puncturer of dreams too rosy to be true. He missed her terribly, although (so far as I could see) without complaint.

I loved and envied the boldness of Ralph's writing travels: two months here or there to write another novel, eat well, and laugh a lot—in Sicily, on Capri, even in Sarasota, Florida.

Ralph lit my life, kept my compass true, ate well with me (mostly I with him), and made me laugh a lot. Not a few times, I kept him from working at his desk, with long telephone calls.

I will never forget founding *Crisis* with him (at first it was *Catholicism in Crisis*). We each put in $2,000 to get the first issue out, and trusted in Providence to bring us enough in the mail to let us put out another one, and another. It always came.

Ralph, dear friend, I cannot say that I will miss you, or grieve for you. I know you are with us, even closer than before. I know that you are laughing at our blunders. And pulling for us. Thanks, good friend.

Michael Novak's website is www.michaelnovak.net. *Among his many books is* No One Sees God. *This contribution originally appeared on thecatholicthing.org.*

Funeral Sermon for Ralph McInerny

"Wisdom," we read in the Book of Ecclesiasticus, "brings up her own sons, and cares for those who seek her. Whoever loves her loves life; those who wait upon her early will be filled with happiness. Whoever holds her close will inherit honor, and wherever he walks, the Lord will bless him." To invoke these words of Scripture seems especially appropriate today when we gather here to pay tribute to the life and mourn the passing of Ralph McInerny. Appropriate too that we should do so within the Resurrection liturgy celebrated in the very church where Ralph—thousands of times, I should think—shared in this deepest of sacred mysteries and ate the Eucharistic bread of the strong. We come, to be sure, to pray for his repose, as is our duty as fellow members of the communion of saints. But we come also to remember one who held wisdom so close and who waited upon her so early that surely the Lord has blessed him. I will cheerfully give you odds that even now he rests in the bosom of Abraham.

The Wisdom that Ralph McInerny so assiduously cultivated left an astonishing literary and philosophical legacy. It would be hard to exaggerate the breadth and depth of his professional productivity. Every day he did his "pages," as he put it, whether a profound examination into analogy or ethics or natural theology, or a piece of serious fiction, or a Father Dowling mystery, or a translation from the French or Latin of some arcane treatise, or perhaps one of his poems—sometimes playful, sometimes poignantly personal—or maybe a children's book, or a biographical study of someone like Jacques Maritain, or a sturdy defense of a contemporary figure like the oft maligned Pope Pius XII, or an essay of literary criticism, an art in which, to my mind, he was particularly skillful. And through all these millions of pages—the last composed only months ago—you'll find nary an awkward sentence; instead there shone through them a clarity, a wit, a precision which brings to the reader enlightenment and delight.

But impressive as this partial inventory may be, Wisdom in the biblical sense embraces far more than the quantifiable. Indeed, for Ralph McInerny the early seeking of it began in south Minneapolis during the Great Depression, within the confines of St. Helena's parish, which served, as it still does, largely middle- and working-class neighborhoods. The families were large and boisterous, their Catholic faith straightforward and uncomplicated. Ralph and his numerous and talented siblings developed a set of values which were themselves a species of wisdom, an insight into a real world of hardworking people among whom fulfillment of duty was taken for granted. It was as though the Catholic faith and the American dream melded together to proclaim that the Jeffersonian "pursuit of happiness" was really not different from the Baltimore catechism's insistence that the whole point of human existence was to love God and, ultimately, to be happy with him in heaven. Of course all sorts of nuances suggest themselves, all sorts of exceptions and reservations and doubts. But, even so, a noble grounding was to be found there, in the rich diversity of Catholic family life, played out in a social environment which is now enshrined only in the memory of a generation passing away.

Nazareth Hall has passed away too. Not the large and handsome building dominated by an imposing Norman tower, located on the shores of a lake on the northern outskirts of St. Paul.

But it no longer serves as a preparatory seminary for Catholic teenagers and young men who wanted to discern whether or not they had a calling to the priesthood. Indeed, the Hall is now a center of Evangelical Protestant activity—which is itself a comment on our times. Ralph McInerny wrestled as hard as Jacob did with the angel trying to make up his mind about a religious vocation; during the 1940s he attended Nazareth Hall twice, with a tour of duty with the Marine Corps in between. And after that he spent two years at the major seminary in St. Paul before he came to understand that God had not called him to be a priest. But Nazareth Hall nonetheless left its own form of wisdom upon him. The rather high toned classical curriculum suited him—"a lovely island of humanities" he called it—as did the regularity of the schedule, which left plenty of scope for creativeness in one who discovered a striking verbal facility within himself. As he put it in his Memoir, "This is when I first began to regard myself as a writer—in remote potency, as I would learn to say later."

Anyone who has read Ralph's fiction or some of his poetry has no doubt seen explicit and implicit reference to these years. "Sometimes," he wrote six decades later, "I think that for those of us who did not go on to the priesthood, Nazareth Hall functions as a kind of Garden of Eden, the measure with reference to which all else must be defective. I have never known anyone from my time there who spoke of the place otherwise than in a laudatory way. Those years formed us and furnished our imagination as well as our memory."

Ralph McInerny's brief sojourn at the major seminary in St. Paul put him on track for the kind of wisdom for which he is, I suppose, most famous. A gifted young professor of logic and metaphysics placed in his hands, not the aridities of handbook philosophy so prevalent then in seminary education, but the very texts of Aristotle and Thomas Aquinas. He found in them an unparalleled intellectual excitement. "I was hooked from the beginning," he said. And since the gifted young professor was a recent product of Laval University in Quebec, Ralph was thus drawn into a specific version of the great Thomistic revival, the one dominated and inspired by Professor Charles DeKoninck of

Laval. Ralph never swerved from his devotion to this mentor; in fact his editing and translation of DeKoninck's works in three volumes has been the preoccupation of these last years. DeKoninck is reputed to have been a fellow of considerable discernment; perhaps therefore he would not have been surprised that this pupil of his became the most distinguished Thomist of his own generation.

And then came Constance Kunert. The wise is also the beautiful, and Connie brought a beautiful wisdom into Ralph's life, not only the physical beauty of her person but also the beauty of her steadiness, her tact, her taste, her candor, her loyalty—her love. Luckily for him, Connie was no philosopher; she was above all practical, down to earth, an agent of stability, "my chancellor of the exchequer" he called her, who enabled him to entertain cosmic thoughts rather than be distracted by thoughts about filthy lucre. Their marriage lasted through good times and bad for half a century—the worst time was the death of three-year-old Michael, their first child—and when she was taken from him Ralph in one sense never really recovered. But if ever a man was blessed in his children, that man was Ralph McInerny. He was justly proud of the six of them and of their spouses, and their affection and devotion to him could have been given no better testimony than the loving care they lavished upon him during these last dreadful ten months. This was beautiful indeed.

Ralph came to Notre Dame, our Lady's University, in 1955. Like many of us he could wax nostalgically about his first sight of the campus, his drive down Notre Dame Avenue toward the golden dome. "I was coming home to a place where I had never been," is the way he put it. And over the years since he freely dispensed the wisdom he had struggled to make his own, for his students and his colleagues, lecturing to undergraduates, directing graduate students, administering an institute and a center. In the recent past, however, the place began to feel less like home than it had that day of first arrival. Ralph identified with the Notre Dame of Frank O'Malley and Tom Stritch, of Ed Fischer, Dick Sullivan, and Father Leo Ward. That Notre Dame was gone, a fact which made Ralph uneasy, because he related the change to what he saw as the diminution of the university's unequivocal commitment to the Catholic tradition. And so he became somewhat ambivalent toward the institution— ambivalent, I say, not hostile, not at all, but also, alas, not without a deep sadness.

What then is the ultimate Wisdom? Jesus said, "This is eternal life, to know thee, the one true God, and Jesus Christ whom thou hath sent." I spoke a moment ago about the old Notre Dame of O'Malley and Stritch. But that was also the Notre Dame of John and Jean Oesterle, both Thomist philosophers of the Laval school and close friends of Ralph and Connie. Thirty years and more ago, when John Oesterle lay dying, Ralph, sitting mournfully at his bedside, leaned forward to catch the raspy words: "Very soon," John was whispering, "very soon I shall know all."

I think it not presumptuous to say that now Ralph McInerny knows all.

Fr. Marvin R. O'Connell is Professor Emeritus of History at University of Notre Dame and the author of numerous books including Pilgrims to the Northland: The Archdiocese of St. Paul, 1840–1962, Edward Sorin, Blaise Pascal, *and* Critics on Trial. *This sermon was preached at the funeral service of Ralph M. McInerny at the Basilica of the Sacred Heart at the University of Notre Dame on February 1st, 2010.*

Appendices

BOOKS AUTHORED OR EDITED BY RALPH MCINERNY

Non-Fiction Books

Philosophical Books

1. *The Logic of Analogy: An Interpretation of St. Thomas.* Nijhoff: The Hague, 1961.
2. *From the Beginnings of Philosophy to Plotinus. History of Western Philosophy, Volume One.* Regnery: Chicago, 1963.
3. *Thomism in an Age of Renewal.* Doubleday: Garden City, NY, 1966.
4. *Studies in Analogy.* Nijhoff: The Hague, 1968.
5. Editor: *New Themes in Christian Philosophy Conference Proceedings.* University of Notre Dame Press, 1968.
6. *Kierkegaard: the Difficulty of Being Christian* With Leo Turcotte. University of Notre Dame Press, 1969.
7. *Philosophy from Augustine to Ockham. History of Western Philosophy, Volume Two.* University of Notre Dame Press, 1970.
8. *St. Thomas Aquinas.* Twayne Publishers: Boston, 1977.
9. *Fides quaerens intellectum.* University of Notre Dame Press, 1979.
10. *Rhyme and Reason: St. Thomas and Modes of Discourse.* Marquette University Press: Milwaukee, 1981.
11. *St. Thomas Aquinas.* University of Notre Dame Press, 1982.
12. *Ethica Thomistica.* The Catholic University of America Press: Washington, DC, 1982.

13. *History of the Ambrosiana.* University of Notre Dame Press, 1983.

14. *Being and Predication.* The Catholic University of America Press: Washington, DC, 1986.

15. *Art and Prudence.* University of Notre Dame Press, 1988.

16. *First Glance at Thomas Aquinas: Handbook for Peeping Thomists.* University of Notre Dame Press, 1989.

17. *Boethius and Aquinas.* The Catholic University of America Press: Washington, DC, 1990.

18. *Aquinas on Human Action.* The Catholic University of America Press: Washington, DC, 1992.

19. *God of Philosophers.* Westminster College: Salt Lake City, 1993.

20. *The Question of Christian Ethics.* The Catholic University of America Press: Washington, DC, 1993.

21. *Aquinas Against the Averroists.* Purdue University Press: Lafayette, IN, 1993.

22. *Thomas's Commentary on the Ethics.* Editor. Dumb Ox Books, Notre Dame, IN, 1993.

23. *Thomas's Commentary on 'De Anima.'* Editor. Dumb Ox Books, Notre Dame, IN, 1994.

24. *Thomas's Commentary on the Metaphysics.* Editor. Dumb Ox Books, Notre Dame, IN, 1995.

25. *The Degrees of Knowledge,* Editor. Vol VII, Collected Works of Jacques Maritain. University of Notre Dame Press, 1995.

26. *Aquinas and Analogy.* The Catholic University of America Press: Washington, DC, 1996.

27. *Ethica Thomistica (revised).* The Catholic University of America Press: Washington, DC, 1997.

28. *Thomas Aquinas: Selected Writings.* Penguin Classics, 1998.

29. *Disputed Questions on Virtue by St. Thomas Aquinas.* Translator. St. Augustine's Press: South Bend, IN, 1999.

30. *Vernunftgemässes Leben: Die Moralphilosophie des Thomas von Aquin; übersetzt von Michael Hellenthal/Ralph McInerny.* Münster: Lit Schriftenreihe der Josef Pieper Stiftung; 3, 2000.

31. *Characters in Search of Their Author: The Gifford Lecture Delivered in Glasgow* 1999–2000. University of Notre Dame Press, 2001.

32. *The Very Rich Hours of Jacques Maritain.* University of Notre Dame Press, 2003.

33. *Zagadnienie etyki chrzescijan,* translated by Ryszard Mordarski. Wydawnictwo Antyk: Poland, 2004.

34. *Aquinas.* Polity Press: Cambridge, UK, 2004.

35. *Summa Theologiae of Thomas Aquinas* by John of St. Thomas. Translator. St. Augustine's Press: South Bend, IN, 2004.

36. *Praeambula fide: Thomism and the God of the Philosophers.* The Catholic University of America Press: Washington, DC, 2005.

37. *The Writings of Charles De Koninck Volume One.* University of Notre Dame Press, 2008.

38. *The Writings of Charles De Koninck Volume Two.* University of Notre Dame Press, 2009.

Other Non-Fiction Works

39. *Married Couples and Humanae Vitae.* Faith Guild: New Hope: KY, 1980.

40. *Miracles.* Our Sunday Visitor Publishing Div: Huntington, IN, 1986.

41. *The Catholic Writer.* Editor. Ignatius Press, 1989.

42. *The Catholic Woman.* Editor. Ignatius Press, 1991.

43. *The Mind and Heart of the Church.* Editor. Ignatius Press, 1991.

44. *Modernity and Religion.* Editor. University of Notre Dame Press, 1994.

45. *Let's Read Latin.* Dumb Ox Books, 1995.

46. *What Went Wrong with Vatican II?* Sophia Institute Press, 1998.

47. *A Student's Guide to Philosophy.* ISI Books, 1999.

48. *Shakespearean Variations.* St. Augustine's Press, 2001.

49. *The Defamation of Pius XII.* St. Augustine's Press, 2001.

50. *The Conversion of Edith Stein.* Translator. St. Augustine's Press, 2001.
51. *The Soul of Wit: Some Poems.* St. Augustine's Press, 2005.
52. *I Alone Have Escaped to Tell You: My Life and Pastimes.* University of Notre Dame Press, 2006.
53. *Some Catholic Writers.* St. Augustine's Press, 2007.
54. *Vaticano II: Che cosa e andato storto?* Fede & Cultura, 2009.
55. *Dante and the Blessed Virgin Mary.* University of Notre Dame Press, 2009.

Fiction Books

Novels & Mysteries:

1. *Jolly Rogerson.* Doubleday: NY, 1967.
2. *A Narrow Time.* Doubleday: NY, 1969.
3. *The Priest.* Harper & Row: NY, 1973.
4. *The Gate of Heaven.* Harper & Row: NY, 1975.
5. *Rogerson at Bay.* Harper & Row: NY, 1976.
6. *Romanesque.* Harper & Row: NY, 1978.
7. *Spinnaker.* Gateway Editions: South Bend: IN, 1977.
8. *Quick as a Dodo.* Juniper Press: Notre Dame, 1977.
9. *Le Cavalcade Romaine.* Gallimard: Paris, 1979.
10. *Abecedary.* Juniper Press: Notre Dame, 1979.
11. *The Frozen Maiden of Calpurnia.* Juniper Press: Notre Dame. 1982.
12. *Connolly's Life.* Atheneum: NY, 1983.
13. *The Noonday Devil.* Atheneum: NY, 1985.
14. *Sleight of Body.* Macmillan: London, 1989.
15. *Frigor Mortis.* Atheneum: NY, 1989.
16. *The Nominative Case (Edward Mackin).* Macmillan: London, 1990.
17. *First Farewell.* Little Skellig Press, 1990.
18. *The Search Committee.* Atheneum: NY, 1991.
19. *Easeful Death.* Atheneum: NY, 1991.
20. *Chambre Froide.* Editions Axel Noel: Paris, 1991.
21. *Infra Dig.* Atheneum: NY, 1992.

22. *Case of the Dead Winner*. St. Martin's Press: NY, 1995.
23. *Case of the Constant Caller*. St. Martin's Press, 1995.
24. *The Tears of Things*. St. Martin's Press, 1996.
25. *The Red Hat*. Ignatius Press, 1998.
26. *Murder Most Divine*. Editor with Martin Greenberg: Cumberland House: Nashville, 2000.
27. *Still Life*. Five Star Press: Unity: ME, 2000.
28. *Sub Rosa* (Egidio Manfredi Mystery). Five Star Press: Waterville: ME, 2001.
29. *Murder Most Catholic*. Editor with Martin Greenberg: Cumberland House: Nashville, 2002.
30. *As Good as Dead*. Five Star Press: Waterville: ME, 2002.
31. *Ablative Case*. Five Star Press: Waterville: ME, 2003.
32. *Green Thumb*. St. Martin's Minotaur, 2004.
33. *Third Revelation*. Mass Market Paperback, Jove Division of Penguin, 2008.
34. *Rogerson Emeritus*.

Father Dowling Mysteries

35. *Her Death of Cold*. Vanguard Press: NY, 1977.
36. *The Seventh Station*. Vanguard Press: NY, 1977.
37. *Bishop as Pawn*. Vanguard Press: NY, 1978.
38. *Lying Three*. Vanguard Press: NY, 1979.
39. *Second Vespers*. Vanguard Press: NY, 1980.
40. *Thicker Than Water*. Vanguard Press: NY, 1981.
41. *A Loss of Patients*. Vanguard Press: NY, 1982.
42. *The Grass Widow*. Vanguard Press: NY, 1983.
43. *Getting a Way with Murder*. Vanguard Press: NY, 1984.
44. *Rest in Pieces*. Vanguard Press: NY, 1985.
45. *The Basket Case*. 1st St. Martin's Press: NY mass market edition, 1987.
46. *Abracadaver*. St. Martin's Press, 1989.
47. *Four on the Floor*. St. Martin's Press: NY, 1989.
48. *Judas Priest*. St. Martin's Press: NY, 1991.
49. *Desert Sinner*. St. Martin's Press: NY, 1992.
50. *Seed of Doubt*. St. Martin's Press: NY, 1993.
51. *A Cardinal Offense*. St. Martin's Press: NY, 1994.

52. *The Tears of Things.* St. Martin's Press: NY, 1996.
53. *Grave Undertakings.* St Martin's Minotaur: NY, 2000.
54. *Triple Pursuit.* St. Martin's Minotaur: NY, 2001.
55. *Prodigal Father.* St. Martin's Minotaur: NY, 2002.
56. *Last Things (On Line Access).* St. Martin's Minotaur: NY, 2002.
57. *Requiem for a Realtor.* St. Martin's Minotaur: NY, 2004.
58. *Blood Ties.* St. Martin's Minotaur: NY, 2005.
59. *Prudence of the Flesh.* St. Martin's Minotaur, NY, 2006.
60. *The Widow's Mate.* St. Martin's Minotaur, NY, 2007.
61. *Ash Wednesday.* St. Martin's Minotaur, NY, 2008.
62. *Wisdom of Father Dowling.* Five Star Press: Unity, ME, 2008.
63. *Stained Glass.* St Martin's Minotaur, NY, 2009.

Andrew Bloom Mysteries

64. *Cause and Effect.* Atheneum: NY, 1987.
65. *Body and Soil.* Atheneum: NY, 1989.
66. *Savings and Loam.* Atheneum: NY, 1990.
67. *Mom and Dead.* Atheneum: NY, 1994.
68. *Law and Ardor.* Scribner, NY, 1995.
69. *Heirs and Parents.* St. Martin's Minotaur, NY, 2000.

Sister Mary Teresa Mysteries written under the pen name Monica Quill

70. *Not a Blessed Thing.* Vanguard Press: NY, 1981.
71. *Let Us Prey.* Vanguard Press: NY, 1982.
72. *And Then There Was Nun.* Vanguard Press: NY, 1984.
73. *Nun of the Above.* Vanguard Press, NY, 1985.
74. *Leave of Absence.* Vanguard Press: NY, 1986.
75. *Sisterhood.* Vanguard Press: NY, 1991.
76. *Nun Plussed.* St. Martin's Press: NY, 1993.
77. *Half Past Nun.* St. Martin's Press, 1997.
78. *The Veil of Ignorance.* St. Martin's Press: NY, 1998.
79. *Death Takes the Veil and Other Stories.* Five Star Press: Waterville, ME, 2001.

Mysteries set at the University of Notre Dame

80. *On This Rockne*. St. Martin's Press, 1997.
81. *Lack of the Irish*. St. Martin's Press, 1998.
82. *Irish Tenure*. St. Martin's Minotaur, 1999.
83. *Book of Kills*. St. Martin's Minotaur, 2000.
84. *Emerald Aisle*. St. Martin's Minotaur, 2001.
85. *Celt and Pepper*. St. Martin's Minotaur, 2002.
86. *Irish Coffee*. St Martin's Minotaur, 2003.
87. *Green Thumb*. St. Martin's Minotaur, 2004.
88. *Irish Gilt*. St. Martin's Minotaur, 2005.
89. *The Letter Killeth*. St. Martin's Minotaur, 2006.
90. *Irish Alibi*. St. Martin's Minotaur, 2007.
91. *The Green Revolution*. St. Martin's Minotaur, 2008.
92. *Sham Rock*. St. Martin's Minotaur, 2010.

The Rosary Chronicles

93. *The Third Revelation*. Jove Books: NY, 2009.
94. *Relic of Time*. Jove Books: NY, 2009.
95. *Good Knights*. St. Augustine's Press, South Bend, IN, 2010.

DOCTORAL STUDENTS DIRECTED BY RALPH MCINERNY

1. Matthew John Kelly, *The Interpretation of St. Thomas Aquinas of Aristotle, Physica 191a7–8: "The Underlying Nature is Known by Analogy,"* 1963.
2. Laurence T. Murphy, *The Role of Nature and Connaturality in Moral Philosophy According to St. Thomas Aquinas,* 1964.
3. Patrick E. Cavanaugh, *The Doctrine of Assent of John Henry Newman,* 1964.
4. Miriam Therese Larkin, *A Study of Language in the Philosophy of Aristotle,* 1965.
5. Carroll Clay Kearley, *The Non-Eleatic Concept of Being in the Works of Jose Ortega y Gasset,* 1965.
6. James T. King, *The Development of Hume's Moral Philosophy from 1740–1751: The Relationship of the Treatise and the Second Enquiry,* 1967.

7. Sister George Marie Caspar, *Gabriel Marcel's Metaphysics of Integral Human Experience*, 1968.

8. George Arthur Martin, *An Interpretive Principle for Understanding Kierkegaard*, 1969.

9. Daryl John Glick, *Freedom, Destiny and Philosophy: An Examination of Blondel's L'action*, 1969.

10. Eugene Carr Buckley, *A Philosophical Treatise Concerning Certain Mathematical Aspects of the Rule of the Majority*, 1969.

11. William H. Bruening, *The Naturalistic Fallacy and Value Terms in Ethics*, 1969.

12. Bahram Jamalpur, *God and Man: A Historical and Critical Comparison of Ibn Sina and Molavi within the Esoteric Iranian Tradition of Islamic Philosophy*, 1971.

13. Donald Henry D'Amour, *Aristotle on Heroes*, 1971.

14. Ralph Henry Johnson, *The Concept of Existence in the Concluding Unscientific Postscript*, 1972.

15. Roderick P. Hughes, *The Notion of the Ethical in Kierkegaard*, 1973.

16. Kerry J. Koller, *Christianity and Philosophy According to Kierkegaard's Johannes Climacus*, 1974.

17. Dolores M. Clarke, *Moral Dispositions in Kant's Ethics*, 1974.

18. James Gillon, *Hegel's Phenomenology of Mind: A Critical Commentary*, 1975.

19. Theresa H. Sandok, O.S.M., *Kierkegaard on Irony and Humor*, 1975.

20. Charles Morton Natoli, *Nietzsche and Pascal: Visions of Christianity*, 1976.

21. Francis William Voellmecke, *Moral Reasoning: Aquinas and Hare*, 1976.

22. Kevin Nordberg, *Philosophy, History, and the Crisis of the Modern Age : Unity in the Thought of R. G. Collingwood*, 1977.

23. Thomas Joseph Gerald, *Lessing's Philosophy of Art: A Chapter in the History of Aesthetics*, 1977.

24. Gerard Casey, *Inference, Assent and First Principles in John Henry Cardinal Newman*, 1983.

25. Patricia A. Guinan, *Carthusian Prayer and Hugh of Balma's Viae Sion Lugent*, 1985.

26. Robert George Kennedy, *Thomas Aquinas and the Literal Sense of Sacred Scripture*, 1985.

27. Thomas S. Hibbs, *The Pedagogy of Law and Virtue in the Summa Theologiae*, 1987.

28. Gregory L. Froelich, *Thomas Aquinas on Friendship and the Political Common Good*, 1988.

29. Robert D. Anderson, *Medieval Speculative Grammar: A Study of the Modistae*, 1989.

30. Mary Frances Sparrow, *The Praeambula Fidei According to St. Thomas Aquinas*, 1989.

31. Kevin Dean Kolbeck, *The Prima Via : Natural Philosophy's Approach to God*, 1991.

32. Karen M. Kuss, *Obedience as a Virtue: A Thomistic Consideration*, 1991.

33. William Mark Smillie, *Phantasia: In Defense of Thomas Aquinas's Account of Imagination*, 1992.

34. Arthur Hippler, *Impediments to Aristotle's Life-Sciences*. Boston College Dissertation, 1993.

35. Anthony P. Andres, *A Thomistic Definition of the Dialectical Topic*, 1993.

36. Steven John Jensen, *Intrinsically Evil Actions According to St. Thomas Aquinas*, 1993.

37. Brian T. Kelly, *Aquinas on Gravitational Motion: An Investigation*, 1994.

38. Thomas DeSales D'Andrea, *The Doctrine of Cause of Being in Aquinas's Summa contra Gentiles : A Case Study in Christian Philosophy*, 1994.

39. Thomas Anthony Cavanaugh, *Double Effect Reasoning: A Critique and Defense*, 1995.

40. Brendan R. Kelly, *On the Nature of the Human Intellect in Aristotle's De Anima: An Investigation into the Controversy Surrounding Thomas Aquinas' De Unitate Intellectus Contra Averroistas*, 1995.

41. Christopher Kaczor, *Thomas Aquinas and Proportionalism: An Evaluation of Their Compatibility*, 1996.

42. John Patrick Thomas O'Callaghan, *Mental Representation: St. Thomas and the De Interpretatione*, 1996.

43. Randall B. Smith, *How the Old Law Shows Forth the Precepts of the Natural Law: A Commentary on Certain Questions Concerning the Law in the Summa of Theology of Thomas Aquinas*, 1998.

44. Timothy L. Smith, *Thomas Aquinas Trinitarian Theology: A Study in Theological Method*, 1999.

45. Michael M. Waddell, *Truth Beloved: Thomas Aquinas and the Relational Transcendentals*, 2000.

46. Raymond F. Hain IV, *Practically Virtuous: Instrumental Practical Reason and the Virtues*, 2009.

47. Patrick M. Gardner, *Dante and the Suffering Soul*, 2009.

Ipse Dixit
(A Few Words from the Honoree)

BALLAD
September 25, 2001

She does not dye her silver hair
But wears it as a crown
And when she gardens in the yard
Or roars across the lawn
Going blade to blade with grass
Her flesh is golden brown.

No one would guess this lady bears
A burden few could carry
Or that there weigh upon her heart
Conceptions far from merry
Her mien suggests insouciance
Her countenance is unwary

But you and I can read within
And we can see her soul
And there we find the secret hid
Though buried deep as coal
The thought that nothing she can do
But time will take its toll.

On the wide horizon of her mind
There looms a menace grim
A fateful date approaches near
When she must sink or swim

A day that brings a cup to her
That's winking to the brim,

A metaphor of sorts that she
Despite what she appears
Has watched the seasons roll away
And heard the hollow cheers
And now must recognize she's known
Ten and three score years.

The young may mock her tragedy
The wise may wisely smile
Her husband who is scarcely wise
But past that stony mile
Quotes Cicero on growing old
And is as usual vile.

Sometimes she sits upon her deck
And watches golfers play
She hears their cries of glee or woe
Their folly on display
And then despite her better self
In whispers she will say:

'What matters brevity of life
Or length if that should be?"
In short, she finds herself soon sunk
In a morass that she
Had sworn forever to eschew
I mean philosophy.
But as they must to men and women
Large questions will arrive
Though she has fought the tendency
To ask why she's alive
And joked that she'll let what's to be
Bug hornets in their hive.

Throughout her life unwillingly
She's heard such questions put
She's listened to the endless fights
And what is more to boot
Has always known her grandma knew
What these poor fools sought.

She bore her children one by one
Beginning in Quebec
Till like a Roman matron she
With children did bedeck
Herself and whatshisname her mate
Yet was no nervous wreck.

The worm was in the apple though
And she could not ignore
That she no longer rose in wrath
And very seldom swore
At rabbits in her garden since she's lived
Ten years three score.

There may be those who chuckle when
Their birthday is recalled
And there are even merry wives
Denying they're appalled
To find the man they're married to
Is very nearly bald.

When I was young and she was younger
When we were in our prime
The measure of our age did not
Make living seem a crime
But now the shadows lengthen
And shorten up our time.

The thing about a ballad is
It can go on and on

But with a subject such as mine
Its conclusion is forgone
And I will end by saying that
I will always love you, Con.

From Ralph McInerny, *The Soul of Wit: Some Poems* (South Bend, Ind.: St. Augustine's Press, 2005), pp. 45–48.

Dust Abhors a Vacuum

Aunt Lucerne was the only relative Philip and Roger Knight had, so it was perhaps fitting that she should be absolute. Once in the dimly remembered past she may have entertained doubts, but this was long before her nephews came to know her. In their experience, she had always been omniscient, riddled with certainty and usually wrong. She was at her most Olympian on this visit.

She sat enthroned in a straight and unforgiving chair, to the left of the fireplace in which no fire blazed, this having been forbidden by Aunt Lucerne as unnecessary in April.

"The temperature is 33," Philip said.

"Fahrenheit," Roger added. But it was folly to think that Aunt Lucerne's outlook could be influenced by mere facts. Her rounded eye had turned on Roger and her brows lifted.

"You're fat."

"Yes, I am," Roger said cheerfully. "I weigh well over three hundred pounds."

"Good Lord."

"Amen."

"No one in our family is fat," she said, sitting even straighter. To say that Aunt Lucerne was slight of build would have been to sin on the side of charity. To be sure, she had with age begun to shrink and melt, in the usual fashion, but some icebergs make it much farther into southern waters than others. What she meant, Roger decided, was that she did not feel fat.

Her attention returned to the mission that had brought her half a thousand miles to the house of her nephews in Rye, New York. She lifted the shopping bag she had been holding since sailing in unannounced fifteen minutes before. Her hands were in need of a fire (and some hot chocolate as well), but she waived away the suggestion.

"The contents of this bag are an insult."

The two brothers waited. She seemed to expect more of a response.

"You are Philip?"

"I am."

"I am told that you are intelligent."

"Word gets out."

"I am also told that you are a detective."

"Yes."

"Good at puzzles, able to understand odd things?"

"Sometimes."

That established, she turned once more to Roger.

"And you are a Catholic?"

"That's right."

That an overweight Catholic should be related to her by blood was clearly a trial for Lucerne. But the question was relevant. She briskly laid out for them the reason for her visit.

The shopping bag contained the contents of a safe deposit box that had been held in the name of her estranged husband. Their marriage had received its final blow when he converted to Catholicism.

"He said he had 'poped.' I did not know the word. This seemed to give him pleasure. Eventually I caught his meaning. It was the last straw."

"You parted?"

She glared at Roger. "He left." Her tone conjured an image of herself in the doorway, pointing toward the horizon while her disgraced husband skulked off into the sunset. "Since you too have poped," she said, wincing, "I thought that perhaps you might discern some twisted significance in what he has done. Your superstitions plus your brother's brains may make some sense of this." She rattled the shopping bag.

News of her husband's death had reached her only after the fact, not that she meant to suggest that she would have hastened to be at his bedside. "There are some things only God can forgive."

Silence fell. Neither brother was inclined to inquire into the precise nature of their uncle's perfidy. Neither had either of them met the man. Since separating from him, Lucerne herself had neither seen nor talked with her husband, Fergus. When she heard that he had left instructions that a key to a safe deposit box be given to her, Lucerne had felt faint stirrings of the milk of human kindness.

"One reads of deathbed repentance, I imagined this was a case of it. The key arrived. The box was in a bank of the city in which I live. Minneapolis," she added, peering at Philip.

"Minneapolis," he repeated.

"Actually, Edina. A suburb."

"So you went to the bank?"

She ignored Roger. She was not to be hurried through her narrative. She was clearly intent on telling them in such a way that it would be unnecessary to go over painful matters again and again.

Admitted to the vault and eventually left alone with the box that had been removed from its place and put on a table where she might inspect it, she had felt the significance of the moment. A faint tremor passed through her body. Less loathsome memories of her spouse assailed her. Almost, she remembered having some smidgen of affection when she consented to Fergus Tracy's pleas and agreed to become his wife.

The corners of her mouth had dimpled with the promise of a smile and then she lifted the cover of the box.

"It was one final insult, from beyond the grave," she cried, the ignominy of that moment returning in full force.

"What did you find?" Roger asked.

"It is all here. As soon as I recovered, I scooped the contents of the box into this shopping bag lest anyone see what Fergus had dared do to me."

"And you have brought everything to us?" Philip said. His eye was on the shopping bag and Roger recognized a more than

professional curiosity in his brother's eye. From time to time
they had spoken of Aunt Lucerne but always in a negative vein.
After all, she had responded to a Christmas card with a note
that they need never again bother to visit such sentimentality
on her. Roger continued to send her a card nonetheless. She
wrote to tell him that she had little money and that in any case
it was already destined to go elsewhere. Reliving their aunt's
humiliation in the bank vault when she opened the safe deposit
box warmed Phil almost as much as a good fire in the hearth
might have.

"Take it," she cried, holding the bag at arm's length.

Philip went for it. Roger was on his feet and at his brother's
side when he pulled aside the bag's handles to look inside.

"A cheesehead?" Roger asked.

"And a piggy bank," Philip noted.

"It is empty," Lucerne said with a disdainful and ladylike snort.

Philip removed what Roger had called a cheesehead, a
triangular piece of yellow plastic made to look like cheese and
worn as hats by fans of the Green Bay Packers. He turned it
over, shook it, smelled it, looked at Roger, and surrendered it to
him. Roger put it on the table. There seemed nothing distinctive
about the unusual headgear: There were doubtless thousands
and thousands identical to it.

The piggy bank was a promotion item from a Green Bay bank,
a rotund ceramic porker wearing a beatific smile with a slot on
its back. On one side was lettered "Mac Livid." On the opposite
side was a piece of masking tape on which was lettered, "Your
name." The triangular sides of the headgear were blank.

"Who is MacLivid?" Philip asked.

"If I knew that I would not be here."

"Have you called this bank?"

She inhaled through her nostrils in a protracted way, seeming
to inflate with the activity, her eyes closed as if in pain. "I must
have an intermediary. You must see how foolish I would look
making such inquiries about an empty piggy bank."

"But there has to be some reason for passing these things on
to you."

"Of course there is. He imagined me calling that bank and asking foolish questions, doubtless causing a flood of gossip about the grasping widow. You must do it for me."

"So you are convinced that these things mean something?"

"I am convinced of nothing of the sort. More than likely it is a practical joke, meant to mock me. I will not give Fergus that satisfaction, not even posthumously."

"How long can you stay, Aunt?"

"How long will it take?"

"That is difficult to say."

"But you think you can find out what it means?"

"I can try," Philip replied and there was a barely suppressed chuckle in his tone. Roger feared that his brother would take culpable pleasure in prolonging their Aunt Lucerne's suspense.

"She is torn between two possibilities," Philip said later when Aunt Lucerne had consented to stay with them and had gone up to the guest room.

"Like Buridan's ass," Roger murmured.

"Don't be unkind."

Roger tried to explain the allusion, but Philip was turning over the cheesehead and inspecting the piggy bank, a grin on his face.

"I wish we had known Fergus better, Roger."

"We didn't know him at all."

Philip regarded the point as pedantic. "MacLivid," he said, reading the side of the pig.

"Any idea what it means?"

"Probably nothing. The old girl may be right. It's just his way of getting back at her."

Roger considered the likelihood of such posthumous vindictiveness and ranked it slight. Aunt Lucerne had asked Philip if he was good at solving puzzles and grasping the point of obscure things. She must have known her husband as well as anyone and found it difficult to accept the theory that this was merely a practical joke.

Aunt Lucerne was without comment on the excellent dinner Philip had prepared and afterward remarked that television gave

her a headache. She settled down with a book written to help
its readers achieve a higher estimate of themselves, a singular
waste of time in her case. Roger repaired to his computer and
soon was happily in communication with his peers throughout
the world. A child prodigy, Roger had received a doctorate
from Princeton at the age of 21. It was at Princeton that he had
converted to Catholicism. A teaching career failed to open up for
him: He was eccentric, putting on more weight daily, and had a
childlike innocence that caused people to doubt that he was as
brilliant as his dossier suggested. An unemployable genius. He
settled down with Philip who, after several muggings, decided
he would conduct his private investigation business from the
redoubt of Rye, advertising an 800 number in the yellow pages of
directories about the country and taking only jobs that promised
diversion as well as money. Roger applied for and received a
private investigator's license and they had become partners
of a sort. Roger was left with considerable leisure to read and
carry on exchanges over the Internet with a far-flung circle of
electronic pals.

Philip went to Green Bay and made inquiries at the bank
that had given out the piggy banks some ten years before.
The director fondled the pig as if a prodigal had come home.
MacLivid? He knew no one of that name. What did he make of
the lettering on the piggy bank's side? He was a stolid man, in
Philip's description, a man whose imagination was not given
much exercise. With reluctance he let Philip inspect the records
of holders of safe deposit boxes. There was none in the name
of Fergus Tracy and none in the name of MacLivid.

"Did you try the Mc's as well as the Mac's?" Roger asked on
the phone.

"Of course."

Philip returned unsuccessful from his trip to Wisconsin. Aunt
Lucerne had trouble controlling her contempt.

"And you call yourself a detective?"

"I think you are withholding information from me."

She fell back in her chair, her mouth agape.

"Withholding information. About those ridiculous items? I know no more about them than you do, apparently. I was right, you see. It is merely a stupid, mean-spirited joke." She whacked her thigh with her self-help book. "I wish I had never come."

She planned to leave the following morning. It was during the night that Roger had his epiphany, whether sleeping or waking he was not sure. But the solution to the riddle Aunt Lucerne had brought suddenly seemed as obvious as could be. He told her this at breakfast.

"I don't want to talk about it."

"Your name means your name."

"What?"

"Lucerne."

"Lucerne means Lucerne?"

"You put Lucerne in the spot covered by the tape saying 'Your name.'"

"What on earth for?"

"The cheesehead," Roger said patiently. "It is Swiss cheese."

"Lucerne, Switzerland?" Philip asked. "You think there is someone named MacLivid in Lucerne?"

"I doubt it very much."

"But MacLivid is lettered on the pig."

"Numbered, not lettered. I think he was using Roman numerals.

Mouth still open, Aunt Lucerne looked from one nephew to the other, as if she had fallen among idiots. They were trying to establish the numerical equivalent of MacLivid.

"Forget the 'A' after the initial 'M.' He presumed we would substitute 'Mc.'"

"One thousand one hundred."

"Eleven hundred," Roger agreed. "But it is a jerry-built construction. I think it means 1154499."

"And what does that mean?" Aunt Lucerne said, but she was unable to retain her note of indignation.

"It means that I have to take a long trip," Philip said.

Roger was left to entertain Aunt Lucerne, who wanted him to go over the interpretation of her inheritance again and again.

Each time he explained, she shook her head as she listened. "It doesn't make sense."

"It's a riddle."

"Fergus was mean, but he was not capable of anything as complicated as this."

"It's not complicated."

She turned down her mouth, as if she thought Roger were congratulating himself.

"I'll bet your brother will find a Mr. MacLivid."

"You mean Monsieur MacLivid. Or Herr. Maybe even Signore MacLivid."

Aunt Lucerne tuned him out, going back to her book. Roger had managed a peek at its contents. Its chapter titles suggested a diffidence foreign to Aunt Lucerne. Don't Undersell Yourself. You're Right Until You Say You're Wrong. Ten Tips on How to Win Arguments. Among the ten Roger found: Never concede. Be aggressive. He began to think that his aunt had written the book.

Two days later Philip called long distance from Switzerland. Aunt Lucerne had snatched up the phone.

"What do you mean, Bingo?"

"Roger was right."

"You found a Mr. MacLivid."

"Is Roger there?"

"I'm on the other phone, Phil."

"It was the number of a safe-deposit box, but it was also the name in which the box had been taken out."

"Did they let you see what was in it?"

"No, but they let Mr. MacLivid."

"And we are now talking to him?"

"Aunt Lucerne, are you still on? There was a message with the money."

"A message?"

"'Put this in your piggy bank.' That's the message."

"You say there's money?"

"A great deal of money."

"But how much?"

"Enough to fill a piggy bank."

When Roger came back to the living room, his aunt sat with her hand still on the hung-up telephone, wearing a stunned expression as she stared at the fireless grate. When she became aware of Roger's presence, she turned and looked sharply at him. But then the expression faded and she looked at him almost with fondness.

"Fergus was a good man."

"I hope he didn't steal the money."

This sent her into an extended fit of agitation, but soon she had convinced herself that her dear Fergus would not do anything either unethical or illegal.

She professed to find it endearing that he had made over his money to her in so oblique a manner.

"Well, what good is an empty piggy bank?" Roger asked.

Her eye roved over nephew's expansive self and a cutting remark seemed to form itself on her lips. But she forbore scolding him.

"What good indeed?"

From Ralph McInerny, *Good Knights: Eight Stories* (South Bend, Ind.: St. Augustine's Press, 2010), pp. 15–26.

Why I Am a Thomist

Ralph McInerny

1

I might begin by listing the teachings of St. Thomas that led me to become a disciple of such a master, but I don't think that would be quite Thomistic since it would make the thing seem an exercise in pure reason. Reason rides on lots of things, not least the quite human context in which, as a fledgling, one is first introduced to philosophy. In a maxim Thomas liked to quote, a line from Aristotle, *oportet addiscentem credere: the learner must trust his teacher.* Of course there are teachers and teachers, and one may come to think his trust was misplaced. For all that, there seems no way around the maxim, at least in the normal course of events.

In his *De magistro* Thomas distinguishes between learning and discovery. Absolutely speaking, one does not need a teacher. Each person is naturally equipped with principles and a kind of rudimentary logic which, in conjunction, can lead him to discover hitherto unknown truths. For the Kant of *What is Enlightenment?* this is the only respectable way to acquire knowledge, that is, on one's own, without reliance on any authority. The disadvantage of this is that everyone would have to invent the wheel for himself. And geometry. And everything else. Presumably being guided by the *Elements* of Euclid is to regard him as an authority and thus to deliver oneself into the hands of another. All in all, Kant's rigorous prescription is at least impractical; it certainly had no counterpart in Kant's own pre-critical intellectual life.

The analogy Thomas draws is that between healing and being cured. The human organism has the wherewithal to heal itself; scratches disappear, for example, and minor flesh wounds, stomach aches, many of the ills that flesh is heir to, but even in the instances where the body can restore itself, medicine speeds up the process. A wound that is closed and bandaged heals more quickly and with less of a scar. This is the native habitat of the phrase *art imitates nature.* The medic by his ministrations helps nature do her stuff more quickly and efficiently. And medicine can correct things nature cannot – broken arms, cataracts, appendicitis. If one went through Kant's essay substituting "health" for "knowledge" and read it as a plea for everyone to be his own doctor it would be even more obvious that it is wildly hyperbolic.

So too the teacher imitates nature, that is, leads the learner more surely and quickly along the path to truth than he could go on his own, and takes him far beyond what he might have discovered even if he had a life as long as Methuselah. But you will say that the authority of the teacher is only an expedient. It is a ladder meant to be taken away when one has a good grip on the brush of understanding. And that is true. But the reminder is a reminder as well of the prior dependence on the teacher. How can one free oneself from holding things because they have been taught him and come to hold them simply because they are true if he had not first tentatively accepted them? Augustine, in his *De magistro*, tells us that we do not send our sons to school to find out what the teacher knows. But send them to school we do in the trust that eventually they themselves will know. Learning is a social and hierarchical thing. Success is had as one gradually frees himself from dependence on the teacher.

Think of how this puts us at the mercy of contingency and of the accidental. Whoever chose his first teacher? If how we begin the study of philosophy is crucial—and who would think otherwise?—the recognition that our beginning could so easily have been otherwise can send a little *frisson* through us. This is but a special instance of the general ineluctable fact, curiously often forgotten, about being human: We are not born adults. For years and years we are in the hands of others—mothers, fathers, babysitters, mean aunts, the Murdstones, and so on. Who has not been set thinking by the first chapter of Book Two of the *Nicomachean Ethics*?

With the distinction between intellectual and moral virtues established, Aristotle asks how the two kinds of virtue are acquired. The former, he says, owes both its birth and its growth to teaching, "for which reason it requires experience and time."[1] Moral virtue, on the other hand, is the result of habit, hence *ethike*, deriving from *ethos*. Moral virtues, Aristotle goes on, do not arise in us by nature, however much natural endowments are their presuppositions. "Neither by nature, then, nor contrary to nature do the virtues arise in us; rather we are adapted by nature to receive them, and are made perfect by habit."[2] Moral

---

1   Thomas, in his commentary, makes this more forceful: "Quae quidem acquiritur nobis magis ex doctrina quam ex inventione" (n. 246). However primary discovery is, learning is the usual way for us; *doctrina* presupposes the capacity for *inventio*, but being taught is more common than discovery.

2   "Sed moralis virtus fit ex more, idest ex consuetudine.Virtus enim moralis est in parte appetitiva. Unde importat quamdam inclinationem ad aliquid appetibile. Quae quidem inclinatio *vel* est a natura, quae inclinat in id quod est sibi conveniens, *vel* ex consuetudine quae vertitur in naturam, Et inde est quod hoc nomen 'morale' sumitur a consuetudine parum inde declinans. Nam in graeco *ethos* per E breve scriptum, signat morem sive moralem virtutem. *Ithos* autem sciptum per H graecum quod est longum, significat consuetudinem. Sicut etiam apud nos nomen moralis significat quandoque consuetudinem, quandoque autem id quod pertinet ad vitium vel ad virtutem" (247).

virtues are acquired by performing acts of an appropriate kind, by accustoming ourselves to act in this way as opposed to that whenever we feel desire or anger. But how can we perform virtuous acts if we do not yet have virtue? That is where parents and other elders and the customs of the country come in. "It makes no small difference, then, whether we form habits of one kind or of another from our very youth; it makes a very great difference, or rather *all* the difference."[3]

What if we had been born into the family next door, rather than into our own? What if we had been born in another part of the city, the state, the country, the world? What if we had been born a thousand or more years earlier, or later? How contingent on so many such things is our outlook on the world and ourselves, and how unlikely that we would ever shuck it all off and begin on our own and *ab ovo*. Indeed, how impossible.

Philosophers of course imagine such fictional beginnings. Wipe your mind clean, make it a *tabula rasa* again, and begin rationally. Ignore the fact that you are writing in French or Latin and all the dependencies that suggests and ask what do I *really* know?[4] Such suggestions, like reading *Robinson Crusoe*, are exciting, of course. What if I were alone in the world? What if everything were different than it is? To respond to such suggestions requires various kinds of sleight of hand, unwitting no doubt, but whose pulse has not sped up at the possibility?

A certain kind of anthropologist, noting our dependence on the milieu into which we happen to be born, and noticing the vast differences in outlook between various cultures, will conclude that our convictions are a function of our milieu, mileux differ, and thus that any traffic across cultural lines is unlikely. Of course he himself is engaged in such traffic, but never mind. The point is of the first importance. Even translation from one language to another seems impossible, as Quine argued—in the English,

---

3   "... non parum differt, quod aliquis statim a iuventute assuescat vel bene vel male operari; sed multum differt, quin potius totum ex hoc dependet. Nam ea quae nobis a principio imprimuntur, firmius retinemus" (254).

4   I have always been struck by the quotations in the preface to *The Critique of Pure Reason*, even in *What is Enlightenment*? Poets, for the most part, but they are invoked as authorities.

Spanish and French versions of his work. Our common humanity seems buried beneath a vast variety of cultural and linguistic overlays and digging it out is not the task of a summer's day. And yet how common, how inescapable, is the assumption of our common humanity?

You have become impatient. I began by speaking of the learning of philosophy and I have wandered off into texts concerned with the acquisition of moral virtue, and this after having drawn attention to the difference between intellectual and moral virtues. But there is a connection. Thomas asks whether teaching is a theoretical or practical activity.[5] He distinguishes between the two things involved, the what of it and the transmitting, and the second he regards as an instance of the active, not the contemplative, life. There is an art of teaching and the end of any art is an activity. All that is obvious enough, to which can be added that there are moral virtues attendant on the art of teaching. And on the side of the learner as well there are moral virtues that characterize the life of learning, and vices to be avoided.[6] So it is that, without confounding the what—say, a truth of geometry—and how best to convey it to the learner, we acknowledge that teaching and learning are transactions that involve far more than the speculative intellect. The success of the process is had when little Orville gets the point and, on his own, is able to show why the sum of the internal angles of a triangle is equal to two right angles.

Furthermore, we become accustomed to the truths we learn and this can prove dangerous. Enamored of the austere discourse of geometry, we might demand that the same method be used regardless of the subject matter. Or, our spirit lifted by poetry, we might demand that all discourse drop into poetry. Of course I am thinking of *Metaphysics*, Book Two, chapter three.

> The effect which lectures produce on a hearer depends on his habits; for we demand the language we are accustomed

---

5   *Q. D. De veritate*, q. 11, a. 4.
6   See *IaIIae*, qq. 166 and 167, on *studiositas* and *curiositas*, respectively.

to, and that which is different from this seems not in keeping but somewhat unintelligible and foreign because of its unwontedness. For it is the customary that is intelligible. The force of habit is shown by the laws, in which the legendary and childish elements prevail over our knowledge about them, owing to habit. Thus some people do not listen to a speaker unless he speaks mathematically, others unless he gives instances, while other expect him to cite a poet as witness. And some want to have everything done accurately, while others are annoyed by accuracy. . . . Hence one must be already trained to know how to take each sort of argument, since it is absurd to seek at the same time knowledge and the way of attaining knowledge; and it is not easy to get even one of the two (994b31–995a14).

Out of such considerations arose the *ordo addiscendi*, laid out succinctly in Thomas's preface to his commentary on the *Liber de causis*.

All this as background for realizing the contingencies attending on the way in which we were introduced to philosophy, studying first St. Thomas and Aristotle. Over those early years of study, we learn a thing or two, but we are also acquiring habits of expectation with regard to any discourse that bills itself as philosophical. We will be attracted or repelled because of what we are used to. This is not something peculiar to fledgling Thomists; it is the common lot of students of philosophy. Hence the enormous difficulty of communication with others whose training has been different from our own.[7]

We did not first survey and assess the varieties of philosophy and then select one of them as our own. No one did or could. We are already into philosophy when we become aware of that

---

7   These matters were first borne in upon me during Vatican II when so
     many who had hitherto called themselves Thomists abandoned the
     dreams of their youth and took up phenomenology or analytic philosophy,
     existentialism, whatever. Alas, their motives seemed mixed. They came to
     regard Thomism as outmoded and wanted to join the forces of supposed
     philosophical progress. In *Thomism in an Age of Renewal* (1965), you will
     find contemporaneous reflections on this tumultuous situation.

variety. And not only a variety of philosophies, but a variety of approaches to each of them. We find that not only are there ways other than Thomas's of doing philosophy, but there are even different Thomisms! And we were introduced to only one of them. This problem—and let no man call it minor—takes me on to my second general consideration: Thomism, not as a habit, but as a network of truths.

2

Pope John Paul II, in his remarkable *Fides et Ratio*, establishes at the outset a way of dealing with the various "philosophical systems," the number and variety of which can seem to prevent any communication between them. This has been called "the scandal of philosophy." Prior to such formal systems, the Pope suggests, and presupposed by any and all of them, is what he calls an Implicit Philosophy. This consists of answers to the great questions which no one can fail to ask, questions which are constitutive of philosophizing, questions that arise out of wonder. Who would doubt that such questions as "What does it all mean?" "What is the purpose of life?" "Is there life after death?" "How can we distinguish good from evil?" are posed by anyone in one form or another at one time or another? What is distinctive of the Pope's reflections is his contention that not only are such *questions* common to all, but that there are *answers* to them which are common to all, and those answers make up what he calls Implicit Philosophy. (n. 4)

When he sets forth those common answers, the reader will be struck by their Thomistic tone. Is the Pope suggesting that Implicit Philosophy is equivalent to Thomism? Not at all. Rather, this implicit philosophy is presupposed by every philosophical system, Thomism and all the rest. Furthermore, it provides a means of appraising and ranking those systems. One who does formal or explicit philosophy will reflect on its presuppositions and therein I find the peculiar attraction of the thought of St. Thomas. He insists that there are principles or starting points of both theoretical and practical thinking that everyone already knows and he spends a lot of time articulating and analyzing them. Those principles are self-evident or nongainsayable truths which are formally considered at length in *Metaphysics IV* and in the Treatise on Law. The *accounts* of such principles occur within what we may call, following the Pope, the philosophical system Thomism, but they are accounts of what it and any system presupposes.

A remark that Thomas cites with approval is that a small mistake in the beginning becomes progressively greater as one goes on from it. What over the years has struck me about Thomas is the way in which his philosophizing is always in warm connection with those pre-philosophical starting points. If later lofty and recherché discussions cannot be brought back to those beginnings, something has gone wrong. This may not make Thomism unique, but it certainly separates it from systems that begin by calling into question, doubting, seeking to lay aside, those starting points. That counts against them, whatever else of value, despite that beginning, we may find in them.

I repeat: the great and abiding attraction of Thomas is the way his thinking is always linked to the principles or starting points, that is, with what everyone already knows. Untutored by a jaded skeptic, everyone knows that there is a world in which things change and move, come into being and cease to be. Give a name to them all; they are natural things, physical objects. That is where Thomas begins, with an analysis of physical things, of things that come to be as the result of a change. Out of that analysis the whole of his philosophy organically grows, and in that sense surely we can call it a system. Thomas's commentary on Book One of the *Physics* and his derivative *De principiis naturae* provide the *sine quibus non* of everything in his philosophy, and in his theology as well. Yet I have heard people groan at the mention of the so-called hylomorphic theory. Shame on them.[8] Who can ponder the texts I have mentioned and not feel the sheer joy of

---

8   Such groans are often prompted by the unwarranted assumption that all
     truths about the natural world are deliverances of experimental science
     and thus that the philosophy of nature of Aristotle and Thomas must be
     consigned to the great dust bin of history. But it is just that assumption that
     must be exorcized.

philosophizing, the *gaudium de veritate*? There is nothing in the mind or in language that does not derive first from the senses.

A few years ago, in a little book called *Aquinas*[9], so far overlooked by the Nobel Committee, I sought to lay out schematically but persuasively how everything later in the philosophy of nature, in talk of the soul, in analyses of sensation and intellection and on into metaphysics comes out of that initial analysis as the whole of Russian literature is said to come out of Gogol's *Overcoat*. *Nihil in intellectu quod non prius fuerit in sensu.* One relishes such Latin phrases, doubtless due to habit, but not only due to habit. One thanks God that he began philosophizing under the guidance of Thomas Aquinas.

Of course there were middle men. My first professor of philosophy was a recent graduate of Laval; I went on to study under the incomparable Charles DeKoninck.[10] Along the way, I became aware that there were different approaches to Thomas than DeKoninck's. I have weighed them and found them wanting. I am by training and conviction a Laval Thomist, that is, an Aristotelian-Thomist.

To describe oneself thus, as a sub-species of one of the many competing philosophical systems, may seem risibly narrow. And of course it could be. One might have confined himself to assimilating Thomas Aquinas and wished a pox on all the other philosophers. But this would be decidedly un-Thomistic. How many of the various ways of doing philosophy make it an obligation to consider *nihil philosophiae alienum*? But so it is with students of St. Thomas. One need only consider the reasoning behind the Church's repeated recommendation of Thomas Aquinas, to say nothing of Thomas's own practice, to see why this is so.

Thomism is a kind of Christian philosophy. That is, it is undertaken and carried on in the ambience of the faith. Everyone's philosophizing is begun and carried on in some

---

9   *Aquinas*, in the collection Classic Thinkers, Polity Press, Cambridge, 2004.

10   The first and second volumes of *The Writings of Charles DeKoninck*, edited and translated by Ralph McInerny, have appeared from the University of Notre Dame Press. There is a projected third volume.

existential ambience, often not reflected on. The Catholic is, whether he realizes it or not at first, following the guidance of the Church when he begins philosophizing with Thomas Aquinas. Philosophy is philosophy, of course, but philosophizing that is Christian is always on the *qui vive* for the way in which what we can know relates to what we believe. And what we believe is not the private possession of a few; it is a common good addressed to all. It is the truth that frees. Philosophical positions that collide with the faith will draw the attention of Thomists, but their interest in whatever is or has been done in philosophy is grounded in the conviction that there is something valuable in any sincere effort to gain the truth. Faith and reason are not only compatible, they are mutually reenforcing.

We live in changing times, as Adam said to Eve on the way out of the garden. Once foes of Thomism attacked it because it was false, and provided arguments that could be countered. Now there are many philosophers who do not regard even their own philosophy as true in any robust sense. There is nothing to which our judgments could conform that might render them true, or collide with and thus be exposed as false. There is no there there, at least that we can get to. We are enclosed in the cocoon of our language or thoughts. Protagoras, call your office.

More than ever now we must concentrate on the very starting points, the truths that are nongainsayable. If objections to them are allowed to stand, the whole edifice will seem to collapse. And, as Aristotle added, the young will be dispirited. Such seemingly small victories seem to be the desideratum of the day. The reach of reason must be defended, its capacity to know and to attain truth. This is of supreme philosophical importance. Why else did Plato and Aristotle devote so much attention to the Sophists? To the principle of contradiction? But it has the further importance that, if reason's ability to arrive at truth is questioned, faith which builds on reason will be undermined as well. It would be impious of us to permit such undermining.

This essay, one of Ralph's final scholarly contributions, appeared in Summer 2009 in the American Catholic Philosophical Quarterly, *a journal he once edited when it was called* The New Scholasticism.

Mementoes Never Die

Ralph McInerny

They show up often in books, unintended reminders of something that is very likely no business of the discoverer's. In his novella, *Kathleen*, Christopher Morley gets the action going when a young man finds a letter in a book. *Letting Go*, Philip Roth's best novel, I think, begins with a young man reading a letter from his dying mother and the reader is caught up in its elegiac phrases and the poignancy of such communication between parent and child.

Old missals and breviaries are often veritable files for holy cards, among them memorials of someone's death. Someday in the unimaginable future someone will open a book and find such a card. "In Loving Memory of Mary Elizabeth O'Callaghan. December 10, 1996." That single date will set the mind going and something at least generic about sadness and hope will be stirred up in another soul.

At protest against the centrifugal force of modern society, there is much talk of families and communities, most of it bogus. Real families become tenuous and unstable and individuals seem only that, individuals. But there is only one way in this world and that is via a mother's womb; birth is to that degree a social event. "For we are born in others' pain, and perish in our own."

If death is something each must do alone, it also involves others, and never more so than when a child dies, especially in the womb. When Mary and John learned that their child, already seven months along, no longer lived, they were devastated. A delivery without hope of life, the ambiguity of one dead before she saw the light of day. They were fortunate to find that they would suffer their ordeal in the midst of family.

Their own, of course, parents and siblings, but a wider one as well, that of Notre Dame. Just north of campus there is a grouping of buildings: married student housing. There in penury and shared anxieties and joys, young people pursue advanced degrees against a background of domestic noise: kids laughing and crying, the spills and thrills and parties and anniversaries, pregnancies, births, baptisms. In this village, as it has been called for more that twenty years, there had never before been an event like Mary Elizabeth. Always before, miscarriage had occurred early. A still-born infant was new. It was not something to go through alone, and in these circumstances it would have been impossible to do so.

Father David Burrell, the chaplain of the Village, said Mass in the crypt of Sacred Heart Basilica, and it was edifying to see a professor acting as what he more essentially is, a priest. Father Michael Sherwin preached a moving sermon on the way our lives are strung upon the rosary that recalls the mysteries of our salvation. The church was packed. There had been no announcement of the Mass, there didn't have to be. People heard and came. For those who were there, that is what this little card will recall.

But it will fall under the eyes of others down the years. In *La vie spirituelle* of 1938, I came upon a card, bound permanently with the pages of the magazine, a card asking that favors granted by the intercession of an Archbishop should be made known to an address given. Whoever used it as a bookmark scarcely imagined that it would be at least as permanent as the page it marked. Libraries and used book stores are treasuries of such unintended reminders and one hears the ghost of Hamlet's father keening, "Adieu, adieu, remember me."

In a copy of the *Summa theologiae*, I have kept a letter from my mother, a mere bookmark at the time; she was alive then and of course would write other letters. Mothers are immortal. Eventually I realized how precious it was. It bears no date but from its contents I can locate it on the line of her life and ours. In a copy of Thomas's *Quaestiones disputatae*, there is a letter from Marvin O'Connell written when I was a graduate student and he still a seminarian. Thus in books of mine I find notices for faculty meetings that took place decades ago and in a copy of Plato's *Republic*, bought in 1949, I recently found an earnest note to myself in which I laid out the dialogue I would write that would rival Plato's. Ah, youth!

Long thoughts brought on by a sad yet somehow joyful event. There are as many joys and sadnesses as there are lives, many more in fact, and all the more because we are sustained by others when the sadness comes and it becomes in some sense theirs as well. So I recall little Mary Elizabeth as I will always remember Michael McInerny who went to God forty years ago at the age of three and whose wide blue eyes looked into mine from the card I carry in my wallet.

This article first appeared in the February 1997 edition of Crisis.

The Last Written Words of Ralph McInerny as recounted by his brother D. Q. McInerny

It is perhaps common knowledge now, at least within the McInerny family, that just a few hours before his death, Ralph, propped up in bed, asked his son for some writing materials. On the pad given him, Ralph wrote: "**I commend my soul to God**." It was the last thing he wrote in this world, and perhaps, of all the thousands upon thousands of words he had written over the course of his life, these were the most telling. He died early the next morning. It was January 29, the feast of Francis de Sales, the patron saint of writers.

Permissions

Thanks to *First Things* and the Institute for Religion and Public Life for permission to reprint Thomas Hibbs' article "Ralph McInerny (1929–2010)" appearing in the April 2010 issues of *First Things*. Thanks also to the *American Catholic Philosophical Quarterly* for permission to reprint Ralph's article, "Why I Am a Thomist," which appeared first in the Summer 2009 *ACPQ* vol. 83, no. 3. "Ballad: September 25, 2001" is from McInerny's *The Soul of Wit: Some Poems* (South Bend, Ind.: St. Augustine's Press, 2005), pp. 45–48. "Death Abhors a Vacuum" is from McInerny's *Good Knights: Eight Stories* (South Bend, Ind.: St. Augustine's Press, 2010), pp. 15–26. Finally, a word of appreciation to the *Weekly Standard* for permission to reprint Jody Bottom's article, "*Ralph McInerny*, 1929–2010." Vol. 15, No. 21, February 15, 2010. The articles originally appeared on thecatholicthing.org